RYAN GIGGS

My Life, My Story

RYAN GIGGS
My Life, My Story

Ryan Giggs

WITH IVAN PONTING

headline

Dedication

To my family

First published in 2010
by HEADLINE PUBLISHING GROUP

1

Cataloguing in Publication Data is available from the British Library

ISBN 978 0 7553 6142 7

Typeset in Nimbus Sans Novus

Printed and bound in Italy by
Rotolito Lombarda S.p.A.

Headline's policy is to use papers that are natural, renewable and
recyclable products and made from wood grown in sustainable forests.
The logging and manufacturing processes are expected to conform
to the environmental regulations of the country of origin.

HEADLINE PUBLISHING GROUP
An Hachette UK Company
338 Euston Road
London NW1 3BH

www.headline.co.uk
www.hachette.co.uk

Contents

Foreword

by Sir Alex Ferguson

Ryan Giggs is a lovely person, every bit as unassuming and wholesome as he was the first time I met him when he was just a wee slip of a lad, barely embarked on his teens. That was not too long after I had taken over as manager of Manchester United in November 1986 and now, as I look back on his phenomenal career, which has made him the most decorated footballer in the history of the English game, I find it staggering to contemplate that the better part of a quarter of a century has flown by since our paths first crossed.

His achievements have been recognised, of course. His name is wreathed in clouds of glory, his reputation is unassailable, he is an idol to millions all around the globe and he has accumulated enough assorted silverware to fill a phalanx of trophy cabinets. But there is one accolade which has yet to materialise, although I trust it is only a matter of time before it does. How I would love to adorn my teamsheet with the words 'Sir Ryan Giggs'.

And why not? After all, it might be said that Clive Woodward became a knight of the realm essentially for winning three games at the 2003 World Cup. Now, I'm certain that most of England, and everyone on the rugby scene, would say his honour was richly merited, and I wouldn't argue with that. But after making more than 800 appearances for Manchester United, many of them in extremely high-pressure situations, doesn't Ryan deserve it, too? Unquestionably he does, as much as any other sporting figure we have known in these islands.

If it happens there's no doubt that his team-mates will take the mickey mercilessly, but behind all the banter lies absolutely gigantic respect. When we won the Champions League in Moscow and Ryan broke Sir Bobby Charlton's club appearance record on the same night, they made a presentation to him and almost raised the roof as they sang, 'That, Boy Giggsy – he's won the league ten times.'

It was fantastic to see their regard for him, but it didn't surprise me. He's like a god in the dressing room, yet he's never stopped being accessible, he's always ready to help the younger lads with a word of advice. After all that success a lot of people would have rested on their laurels, but not Ryan. His reaction was to play a brilliant part in winning an eleventh league title and to help us reach another Champions League final.

When will he retire? I wouldn't like to take a bet on that. Some people have got such a drive that they never want to stop, and Ryan Giggs is like that. Though he's passed his thirty-sixth birthday, he's as fit as a man can be, and I can see him carrying on for another couple of seasons, at least. I think his form is better now, in 2010, than it was five years ago. There was a period, as he moved into his thirties, when he had a little dip and I think he was starting to worry. He was suffering from recurring hamstring problems. Eventually we discovered that they were coming from his back, and then we found a way to manage them. He started doing special stretches before and after games and training, and doing yoga a couple of days each week. The results have been incredible – he's been like a new man. He's lucky in that he's never carried any weight, which is partly down to his own regime but also it's in his genes.

Then there's the way he handles himself. If you look at Ryan in virtually any situation, he's neither up nor down. Over twenty years I've seldom seen him lose his temper, and that's a big advantage – although some might say I'm a fine one to talk about that! Ryan's a low-key person in the amount of energy he expends on outward emotion. Some people can tire themselves with their talking – for instance, Gary Neville has had a magnificent career, but he's a very emotional guy, which can cost him energy. Ryan never gets to that level, so he's always got something in reserve.

As a footballer, of course, 'That Boy Giggsy' has been nothing short of sublime. The first time I saw him in a trial at the Cliff, our old training ground, my jaw dropped. He just seemed to float over the ground, and I make no apology for repeating my first impression of him because I believe it was so apt – he reminded me of a puppy chasing a piece of silver paper in the wind.

Right from that moment I was sure in my heart that he would make the grade, and nothing happened to change that notion. Pretty soon our chief scout at that time, Joe Brown, and myself started going to see his parents a couple of nights a week to impress on the boy to come to United instead of

> **❝** As a footballer, of course, 'That Boy Giggsy' has been nothing short of sublime. **❞**

City, with whom he'd already done some training. He was always very quiet and shy, but his eyes were bright and a wee bit wide. He's a very intelligent lad and it was as though he was drawing all the knowledge into himself through his eyes. We were such persistent visitors that in the end we were expected, and I shall always remember his mother asking, 'Now, shall we be seeing you again on Thursday?'

If any proof were needed of Ryan's potential, it was afforded when we threw him into a practice match against first-teamers when he was only fourteen. He was up against Viv Anderson and he was unbelievable, leaving Viv gasping 'Who the ******* hell is that?' as he panted along in the boy's wake.

Now it was obvious to all that we had something special on our hands. Apart from his pace and his ability on the ball, what also marked him out were his bravery and his balance. When someone has all those attributes, and an even temperament to go with them, there are no limits to what can be achieved, and it has been a joy to watch him realise every ounce of that vast potential.

What delights me most of all, though, is that Ryan, like Paul Scholes and Gary Neville, is a part of the United family. They have grown up at the club and eventually they will be offered long-term roles. Who understands the club better than lads who have played for us on all the grand occasions? They know what it means to be Manchester United players and I believe they have a massive part to play in the club's future.

In the meantime, I can't wait for Giggsy to hear those three little words: Arise Sir Ryan!

Introduction

I've been a very lucky boy. That's the only rational conclusion I can draw as I cast my eyes over the images gathered together in these pages and reflect on the story of my life and career to date.

It's not as though I always intended to be a professional footballer. I'm not trying to say I'm a frustrated accountant or anything like that; it's more that I never gave the slightest thought to the future as I was growing up as a sports-mad teenager. Even when I signed for United, it didn't occur to me that I would be in the first team so soon and certainly there was no notion that I would go on to realise all my wildest fantasies with the club I had come to adore.

But things kept happening, and happening, and happening. I got into the side, we won the League Cup, then came the Premiership, and then the league and FA Cup double, all in successive seasons and before I had reached my twenty-first birthday.

In all honesty, I'm not a particularly confident person away from football, definitely not the type to be sure I was going to make the grade. But it turned out that when I crossed that white line I felt totally at home, that I had some talent and that I could make the most of it. The upshot has been two decades with the only club I could ever envisage myself playing for.

During that time I've had the privilege of playing alongside dozens of world-class performers, and people often ask me who has been the best. Probably my favourite is Scholesy, but the best? How could you separate Bryan Robson and Roy Keane? Or Eric Cantona and Mark Hughes, Cristiano Ronaldo and Wayne Rooney, Peter Schmeichel and Edwin van der Sar? The list goes on and on.

Then I have had the fabulous good fortune to develop under the watchful eye of Sir Alex Ferguson, surely the greatest manager there has ever been; and I have also been jammy enough to escape serious injury, clearly a key factor in my longevity.

I have made countless lifelong friends during my career – many of them household names, but lots that aren't, too – and I am blessed with a family which is as loving and supportive as it is possible to be.

Now I find myself telling my story through this collection of striking images, which I believe is a tremendous way to involve people and catch their interest. One glance at a photograph is enough to transport the viewer back in time, getting there a lot quicker than by reading any number of words.

For instance, the picture opposite is instantly identifiable as one from the game with Manchester City in February 2008 which marked the fiftieth anniversary of the Munich tragedy. It was a special day and the shirt, devoid of logos, was totally appropriate to the occasion. If someone looks at that shot in thirty years' time they'll know straight away when it was taken. I could think of no more fitting way to start this book.

CHAPTER ONE

Running down the wing . . . for England

⌄ I'm Welsh through and through, and always felt that I'd end up playing for Wales, but I really enjoyed my time as captain of England Schoolboys. It didn't feel strange, why should it? After all, I'd lived in England for nearly ten years, I'd played with four or five of these lads for Greater Manchester and I'd loved every minute of it. It was great fun going to Nottingham for trials and then to Lilleshall, being surprised that I was always picked as the squad was whittled down from one hundred and twenty-five, to eighty, to forty, to twenty-five, and finally to eighteen. The manager was Dave Bushell, who's now a key man in United's youth development set-up, and there was a terrific bunch of lads. That's me, second from the right on the front row with my hand on the trophy which we received for beating Belgium at Wembley in March 1989. Most people will recognise Nick Barmby, who went on to such a terrific career, on the far left of that row, and among others in the picture are Adie Mike and John Foster (fifth and sixth from the left in the back row), who went to Manchester City, and David Hall (fourth from left, same row), who joined Oldham. On the far right of the back row in the tracksuit is Del Deanus, a lovely lad destined for a tragic future. I'll come back to Del a little later.

⌃ This was my first game for England Schoolboys, as a fifteen-year-old against Northern Ireland in Craigavon in March 1989. I was playing for United by then, and I was particularly pleased when we won 4–0. Their skipper was Steve Lomas, who I had trained with at Manchester City. I lined up in central midfield as I did for Salford Boys, and I enjoyed the role because I was involved all the time instead of waiting on the wing for somebody to give me the ball. I was quite tall for my age and was comfortable with the physical demands of the central position. At that point I was still playing rugby, so I never felt intimidated by anything I might encounter on the football field. But I had no regrets about returning to the left wing, where I played my club football for Deans. There were not that many left-footers about, and I was quick, so it was a natural place for me to be.

⌃ Descending the famous thirty-nine steps at Wembley after receiving my medal at the end of England's win over Belgium Schoolboys in March 1989. This is my first taste of mixing with the public as a successful footballer, and I look a tad bemused by it all. I don't think you take in too much at that age. I used to let it all go over my head while I enjoyed the moment.

« Maybe I look the tiniest bit embarrassed by all the fuss as I'm photographed with the trophy in my hands but, honestly, I wasn't overawed by Wembley, even at the age of fifteen. I was captain of the team that had beaten Belgium, I had scored a penalty, I was happy to face the cameras.

As for the experience of performing at the famous old stadium, for all its grandeur I rarely felt comfortable there as a player. The grass was always so lush that it held the ball up, making it difficult for me to dribble. It wasn't so bad as a central midfielder for England because I didn't run with the ball so much, and I must admit that it was a beautiful passing surface. But later, having returned to the wing, I feel I didn't have too many good games at the original Wembley. I prefer it at the new ground, where the feel of the pitch is much more like everywhere else. Sadly in 2010 there have been new problems with the surface which have upset some players and managers.

⌃ This is a genuine rarity – a shot of me lining up for Manchester City. It was taken at City's Centre of Excellence at Platt Lane ahead of my one game for them, against a select eleven. That's me second from the left in the front row, and on my right is Steve Lomas, who went on to play more than 100 times for City before nearly doubling that tally for West Ham. Also in shot is Simon Davies (on my left), who joined United and made the first team, and my friend Terence Stockley (on the far right of the front row), who played alongside me for Deans.

I was always a United supporter and I never really had any feeling for City. I only went there because my manager at Deans, Dennis Schofield, was a City scout and a City fan. He organised it for me to go training with the club but although they treated me really well, somehow I never took to it. There was something about the place I didn't like, and occasionally I would bunk off from a training session, which would earn me a bollocking from Dennis. But all's well that ends well . . .

CHAPTER TWO

1990/91 1991/92

The start of something big

People might consider it hard to believe, but in 1992 when United won the FA Youth Cup, I found it more taxing to play in those games alongside my mates than I did to face the likes of Leeds and Liverpool as a regular member of the first team. Maybe it was because everybody was straining every sinew to prove themselves, to make the big breakthrough. I can't be sure, but what I do know for certain is that lifting the trophy with those lads, the people I was growing up with, was an absolutely fabulous feeling.

Looking at this picture, taken after the second leg of the final against Crystal Palace, it's astonishing to reflect that all of us went on to play league football, though George

Switzer played mostly non-league and competed at a decent level for Hyde United for many years. Usually a smattering of players from a youth team go on to greater things, but this was a truly exceptional group. At the time, I'd say Nicky Butt was the outstanding player. He was a tough boy, never intimidated, and he had bags of talent. As for Paul Scholes, although there was never any doubting his ability, there was a worry then about whether he'd be big enough and he didn't make this team. He's made up for it since, though!

Celebrating, back row left to right, are: Ben Thornley, Nicky Butt, Gary Neville, Simon Davies, Chris Casper, Kevin Pilkington, Keith Gillespie. Front row: John O'Kane, Robbie Savage, George Switzer, me, David Beckham, Colin McKee.

>> You might recognise the lad at my elbow, guarding the trophy's plinth and clutching his medal. I think Becks must have elected himself vice-captain – he always liked the camera! David had always been a bit different, with his clothes and his cars. That's just the way he was. He used to get a bit of stick for his Cockney accent and for being a bit flash, though there was never anything nasty or even the faintest bit malicious in the mickey-taking. He loved football and he loved Manchester United. He was a nice lad and he was one of us.

> **❝ It was a landmark day in my football career, but it certainly wasn't an auspicious one. ❞**

⌄ My debut off the bench. It is March 1991 at Old Trafford and I have just risen to replace the injured Denis Irwin in what turned out to be a dismal 2–0 home defeat by Everton. Denis was playing right back that day, so the Gaffer was forced to shuffle his pack. I think he moved Clayton Blackmore into defence and Choccy McClair dropped into midfield, leaving me to form a dual spearhead with Danny Wallace. What a formidable pair of dreadnoughts we must have looked!

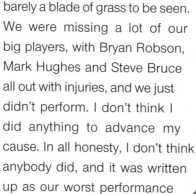

The team was enduring a poor run, and things didn't look up for us that day. The pitch was dreadful, a mixture of mud and sand with barely a blade of grass to be seen. We were missing a lot of our big players, with Bryan Robson, Mark Hughes and Steve Bruce all out with injuries, and we just didn't perform. I don't think I did anything to advance my cause. In all honesty, I don't think anybody did, and it was written up as our worst performance of the season. My most vivid memory of the occasion is of being flattened by big Dave Watson, the Everton centre half. It was a question of: 'Welcome to the big league, young man.' But at least I was up and running.

⌄ It came as a major surprise, the announcement that I was to make my first senior start for Manchester United. It was May 1991 and we were about to face City at home. Our young Australian goalkeeper Mark Bosnich, then in his first Old Trafford incarnation, reckoned he'd heard a whisper that I would be involved, so I thought I might be a sub. When the manager started naming the team, he went through the other ten and then he said, 'Ryan, you play on the left.' I looked around and wondered if I had heard right. I wasn't really paying attention to the starters; I was listening for the two subs (all that were allowed way back then). I recall getting slightly sweaty palms, but nothing more.

When I walked on to the pitch I didn't really feel nervous, not even with City as the opposition. The surroundings were very familiar, as I had played at Old Trafford quite a few times for the youth team. Here I'm confronted by the full back Neil Pointon, and I don't think I look edgy, more totally absorbed in what I'm doing. The fans treated me absolutely brilliantly. Anything I did reasonably well they applauded loudly, and if I missed a pass there was no hint of criticism. I remember feeling at home from the very first whistle.

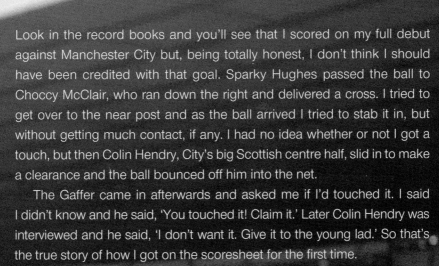

Look in the record books and you'll see that I scored on my full debut against Manchester City but, being totally honest, I don't think I should have been credited with that goal. Sparky Hughes passed the ball to Choccy McClair, who ran down the right and delivered a cross. I tried to get over to the near post and as the ball arrived I tried to stab it in, but without getting much contact, if any. I had no idea whether or not I got a touch, but then Colin Hendry, City's big Scottish centre half, slid in to make a clearance and the ball bounced off him into the net.

The Gaffer came in afterwards and asked me if I'd touched it. I said I didn't know and he said, 'You touched it! Claim it.' Later Colin Hendry was interviewed and he said, 'I don't want it. Give it to the young lad.' So that's the true story of how I got on the scoresheet for the first time.

"It was a proud moment for me to join the senior players for the official club photocall ahead of the 1991/92 season. **"**

» It was something of a coming of age, I guess. There tends to be a lot of messing about on these occasions, and I suppose it can't be easy for the photographers, who are only trying to do their jobs. But I was the youngest one there so I didn't get involved in any of that; I just did what I was told and smiled politely. It's fair to say my approach has changed somewhat down the years!

Back then I thought it might mean that I was in line to be picked for the squad every once in a while, but I would do better than I imagined – getting into the team on the opening day of the season. In the end I made forty-one starts with nine appearances as sub to complete a half-century for the campaign, far more than I had expected.

⌄ Everybody has their favourite grounds, and I have usually enjoyed playing at White Hart Lane, where I haven't done badly as a rule. I don't

suppose it's got anything to do with it, but I think the white shorts and socks – which invariably we wear there to contrast with Spurs' colours – look very smart.

That's Gudni Bergsson on the left and the man challenging me is Steve Sedgley. During this game I had missed a chance – I think I might have shot over from a one-on-one – and was just jogging back when Sedgley said something sarcastic to me. I can't recall the exact words but certainly it wasn't calculated to put me at my ease. I thought to myself, 'Typical Tottenham.' We'd had some battles with them at youth level, and they were regarded as a flashy team that we didn't hold in too much affection. So on this occasion you might say I was a little more delighted than usual when Bryan Robson scored late on to claim all three points.

❯ We were already 5–2 up when I scored this goal at Oldham on Boxing Day 1991, but that didn't spoil my pleasure as I took it round the keeper, Jon Hallworth. They were a decent side at the time, but we just battered them. It was a brilliant team display. I think it was one of the first times I wore a long-sleeved shirt. I found that I just felt more comfortable in it, and I stuck to long sleeves for the next fifteen years or so. Now I prefer short sleeves again, I can't really explain why; it just feels right.

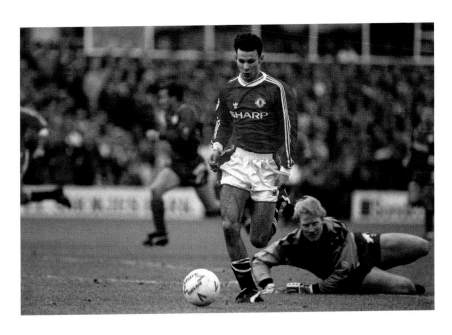

⌃ Paul Ince seems amazed that I've actually managed to put the ball in the net for what proved to be the winner during extra time in the second leg of the 1992 League Cup semi-final at Old Trafford. Me, I'm already turning away to start the celebrations. I was lurking on the right, the ball got knocked across and I just volleyed it back into the far side of the net. I might have shinned it a bit, which possibly accounts for Incey's expression. Certainly I don't think I hit it particularly sweetly, although it finished up in the top corner. Undoubtedly there are times when you score but you actually meant to direct your shot into the opposite corner. If you shin it the poor keeper – in this case the former United man Stephen Pears – hasn't got much chance. After all, if you don't know where it's going, how can he? Regular goal-scorers do that all the time and claim the credit.

This was a big goal because United had never won the League Cup, and had lost the previous year's final to Sheffield Wednesday. It was a huge night for Gary Pallister, too, because he was facing his old club, Middlesbrough, for which he always retained a soft spot. Pally loved the place, went back there at every opportunity, and now he lives just down the road at Yarm.

>> Battling for possession with Liverpool's Ray Houghton on a sunny Sunday afternoon at Anfield, a game that looms large in my memory for all the wrong reasons. It was April 1992 and, even before the match, we had needed a miracle to win what would have been United's first league championship for a quarter of a century. The prize had seemed tantalisingly within our reach until we lost twice in the space of three days to Nottingham Forest and West Ham. We then tasted defeat at the home of our fierce rivals and the dream was well and truly dead.

Not surprisingly, I was feeling absolutely gutted as I walked from the dressing room to board our coach. Even so, when a Scouser approached to ask for my autograph – there was precious little security in those days – I signed for him. Imagine my feelings, then, when he took the piece of paper from my hand, ripped it up and threw it in my face, laughing scornfully and saying, 'You'll never win the league.' Although it was the low point of my career up to that moment, my encounter with that mindlessly crass individual provided brilliant motivation for the future. It happened to several of the lads and the manager used it as a tool, reminding us of the experience and telling us to make sure it never happened again. I was young and naïve, thinking that everyone was my mate, everyone wanted my autograph, but this served to toughen me up. It was a rude awakening to discover just how much those Liverpool supporters didn't want us to succeed. You could feel the hate in the stadium that day and it was personified by that offensive so-called football fan. But in the long term he did me a favour; and he wasn't much of a tipster, was he?

« We might be termed an odd couple, Micky Phelan and myself, as we stroll out at Wembley ahead of the League Cup final against Nottingham Forest in April 1992 – and I don't suppose either of us could quarrel with that description. The suits look pretty sober but the same can hardly be said of the ties. You might say they're rather busy. Have I ever worn mine since? Er, no – I don't know why that is! As for Mick, he was always a snazzy dresser, so he might have picked our striking neckwear.

Looking at this, it's difficult to recognise him as the familiar figure of United's current assistant manager, although it's interesting to see he was already losing his hair all those years ago. Mick has always been a nice lad, though I guess it's fair to say we inhabit different generations, despite the fact that we were team-mates. He used to share rooms with Pally – a weird match because Mick was quiet and Pally wasn't, but they always seemed to get on.

As a footballer, Mick was truly versatile. He would run all day and do a terrific job for the team, whether he was playing in right midfield, centre midfield, at right back or even in central defence. He would never let Manchester United down, then or now.

» I don't know if the referee spotted it, but the camera has caught Denis Irwin grabbing a handful of Gary Crosby's shorts as he gets in a challenge during the 1992 League Cup final. Denis was a gem for Manchester United and it was brilliant for me as a rookie to play directly in front of him when he was at left back and I was on the left wing. I could rely on him totally in every situation. He offered complete stability, rarely

> **"** Denis was a solid, unassuming character and he was exactly the same as a footballer. Pure gold. **"**

missing a game, and whether we were attacking or defending, he was always talking to me, telling me where and when to run. That was exactly what I needed at the time.

Any manager would be glad to have Denis in his side. He was defensively very sound, being in the great United tradition of right-footers who excelled on the left; he could go forward and cross superbly with either foot, and he could score goals. Denis was a solid, unassuming character and he was exactly the same as a footballer. Pure gold.

⌃ League Cup winners for the first time in the history of the club. Look at that beaming grin on the face of Steve Bruce, in the middle of the front row. Right from the beginning of my days at United, Brucie was a massive influence on me. He was always so much fun, so bubbly, but what a warrior! He would play for a whole season with a hernia, or tear his hamstring and be back in ten days. I'd have called that impossible, but Brucie would just rub his leg, grin at the world and on he'd go. 'I was never quick,' he'd tell me, 'so why do I need hamstrings?'

The shirts are certainly an eyeful – although I must admit to quite liking them, despite the disparaging J-cloth comments – but such matters were far from my mind as I celebrated picking up my first senior medal. I was pleased to have set up the only goal of the game against Forest, which Brian McClair scored, and it was good to step away from the pressure of the title race, if only for one afternoon.

STEVE BRUCE:

Ryan Giggs is the most natural footballer I've ever seen. From the day he arrived at United as a fourteen-year-old, you could tell he was something extraordinary, just from the way he moved, the way he could dribble past England right back Viv Anderson in training.

He's always been quiet by nature, and now he's just as modest and unassuming as the day he arrived, despite becoming the most decorated player of them all. That's so refreshing when you see some people having their heads turned by a bit of success. He hasn't forgotten his roots or the need to work and I'd offer him as the supreme example of the way a footballer should live his life.

Despite all he's done he remains fiercely competitive; he still wants to win more honours, and that is the sign of genuine greatness – a word which I don't use lightly. For me, Ryan is right up there with the finest ever, names like Best, Charlton, Law, Cantona and Robson. It's incredible that he's been in the United team for twenty years, an achievement which I believe will never be repeated. There'll never be another Ryan Giggs.

>> What's Sharpie saying? He's probably telling me what we were going to do afterwards. Nobody had a dull time if they stuck with Lee Sharpe. He was my best friend when I first got into the team because we were the closest in age. He was always happy and cracking jokes, and was much more outgoing than me – he's a very confident character, at least on the outside. He was an excellent player, too – like lightning when he was young – though he offered more than raw pace: his crosses were absolutely magnificent.

LEE SHARPE:

Aah, they were good days with Giggsy. We never had a boring night out, that's for sure. He could be quiet at times, but socially he could be very lively. At the time it was a big thing for me when Giggsy came through. The team was full of people in their middle and late twenties, so it was great for me to link up with somebody close to my own age.

We played in the same left-wing position, but we never fell out over that. It was down to the manager to select the team, and often we would swap wings anyway to confuse the opposition. Just look at that speckly blue shirt. We certainly had a few rascal kits, and we used to joke in the dressing room that the designer must have been sniffing glue.

⌃ The first time I was called the new George Best I was only fifteen. I had just been picked for England Schoolboys and I saw a newspaper headline making what can only be described as a very glib comparison. At that point I knew little about George and hadn't even seen film of him playing – in my era the top football heroes were Bryan Robson and Diego Maradona – so it didn't really bother me or play on my mind. Even when I got into the United team, and the George Best thing was raised again, I just let it slide past me. Of course, now that I'm older, and able to appreciate what an incredible footballer he was, I take it as a huge compliment to be spoken of in the same breath as George, even if the words came from the media and the fans rather than people in the game.

When I first met him it was to spend two days making a video with him, and he came across as a lovely character – a natural comedian, very funny, extremely quick-witted, obviously an immensely intelligent man. On this occasion I was being presented with the PFA Young Player of the Year award for 1992. It was after my first full season, and everything seemed to be whizzing past me at full speed, just one thing on top of another. This award was special, though, because it was voted for by my peers, people who knew my game because they played against me.

>> Gary Pallister and I must have cut contrasting figures as we stood at the side of the stage, waiting to be presented with our awards at the PFA ceremony in 1992. I was very young, not in the slightest bit edgy because it was all going over my head. But Pally, who was about to receive the senior award, was really bricking it. He was so nervous about making his acceptance speech that he'd gone white. I can sympathise now because I'd be exactly the same, but at that age I didn't know enough to be jittery.

He might have had a different experience of the evening, but what is absolutely certain is how much he deserved that accolade of PFA Players' Player of the Year. True, after ten minutes of a game he always looked knackered, but that was totally misleading. No one was quicker than him, no one was better than him in the air, and he was great on the ball, being able to ping beautifully accurate passes all over the pitch. Pally was just a top player who should have played more often for England – and he's a top lad, too.

GARY PALLISTER:

Giggsy's right – I was so petrified I could hardly eat my dinner! Brucie and me thought we were only going to make up the numbers, but then we realised none of the other nominees were there and so, by a process of brilliant deduction, we knew that one of us was going to win. Of course, Giggsy was as cool all those years ago as he is now. What a fantastic career he's had, and he still looks the same waif of a lad that he was in 1992. He's one of United's greatest ever, a true legend, and he's handled his fame really well, always remaining level-headed and true to himself. He always loved a laugh, too. We had to watch him, especially when he was with Butty and Scholesy. They were like the Three Amigos. Totally wicked!

CHAPTER THREE

1992/93 1993/94

Getting the taste for titles

> **"** Football has been described as the working man's ballet, and while I have never entertained any delusions about my own style, if the general idea is based on a player's need to run, jump and twist at full stretch when the need arises, then this picture suggests there might be something to the notion after all. **"**

⏋ For me, it is all about pure instinct, as I think is evident from my body shape here. When you have to pull a ball out of the air like this, and drop it dead at your feet, it has to be a natural sequence. There is no way it can be taught.

This shot was taken during 1992/93, the inaugural season of the Premier League, when the shirt with the lace-up collar was introduced. When I first saw it I thought it would be a nightmare, with defenders pulling the laces, but that never happened. As the campaign wore on people came to love it and, because of the success we enjoyed, it has become a classic shirt. I've got one framed at home, the one I wore in the 1994 FA Cup final, a present from Paul Ince.

⌃ It's that word again – instinct. This goal at White Hart Lane in September 1992 came right out of the blue after the Spurs right back, Dean Austin, had been unable to control a long pass out of our defence. I had gambled and was on the spot to take advantage, nipping past him with the ball, then pushing it between the legs of Jason Cundy, who had come out to close me down. Next up was goalkeeper Ian Walker, and I sidestepped him before threading a shot into the net from the corner of the six-yard box.

In this photo, Mark Hughes is waiting in the middle with an expectant expression on his face, but I wasn't tempted to square it to him. It all happened so quickly, I didn't even realise he was there. From the nutmeg to rounding the keeper took just a couple of seconds and I was focused only on the ball. The speed of it is shown by how far back Cundy and Walker are in the picture.

I suppose I was already pretty well known by this time, but the goal really lifted my profile. It was one which people were talking about for the rest of the week; it was nominated for goal of the season; it was included in the *Match of the Day* titles; and it happened in London, so all the press were there.

These are scenes of ecstasy on the magical Old Trafford night in May 1993 when United were crowned as league champions for the first time in more than a quarter of a century. The title had been ours for a little over twenty-four hours, after Oldham had beaten our only challengers, Aston Villa, but the presentation was to take place after our home game with Blackburn.

A few of the lads had, to put it mildly, enjoyed one or two drinks the night before at a party at Brucie's house in Bramhall. When I arrived late, having taken directions off Incey, things were well under way and pretty soon all the lads had turned up. At that point the next day's game against Blackburn was the last thing on our minds, and you might say we enjoyed ourselves to the full. Some of the lads stayed over, but I didn't drink much and got home reasonably early.

When I arrived at Old Trafford for the evening fixture the place was really hopping. My Ford Escort was surrounded by joyful fans jumping up and down. It was almost scary, but nobody was hurt; they were just so, so happy. For everyone who loved Manchester United, it was carnival time.

66 What kept the players going after the night before? Just pure adrenaline. 99

« Kevin Gallacher threatened to spoil the fun by giving Blackburn an early lead, but then we won a free kick about thirty yards from goal. It would have been perfect for Denis Irwin, but for some reason I took it. I just ran up and struck the ball as hard as I could with my left foot. It was glorious to see it go in, then I took off on this crazy sprint to celebrate with Eric.

⌃ It looks a fairly awkward embrace, doesn't it? I was young and it's fair to say I hadn't really perfected my celebrations! It was such a relief to be back on track in the game. We wanted to go out and perform for the fans on such a special day in the club's history. Goodness knows what Eric is saying! Contrary to some people's perceptions, he was very much one of the lads, but there was always that aura of mystery, which was all part of who he was. Certainly Eric had rather more of a command of the English language than he let on to the press. He always knew exactly what was going on.

⌃ Near the end we were 2–1 up, Incey having put us in front; then we got a free kick just outside the box. Pally was our only outfield player without a goal that season – even Paul Parker had scored. In fact, the angle was right for Denis or myself, but then Pally strolled up and said, 'Listen, this one's mine.' Before the game we'd mentioned that if we got a penalty he should take it, but the last thing we expected was for him to come up and slot home a free kick. When it went in we were dumbfounded. We shouldn't have been, considering the way the night had gone. Everyone was chuffed to bits for Pally – it was just the icing on the cake. Here he's looking over to the bench at the manager, who was probably dancing a jig.

GARY PALLISTER:

When we got that free kick, Giggsy, Incey, Denis and Ooh-Aah were all milling about, clearly fancying it. But, just that once, I had to lay down the law. There was no way I wasn't having that one. Afterwards I think young Giggsy was lost in admiration. He was hanging off me at the celebration – probably asking for a few tips!

>> Do that jacket and tie match? Er, no! It was a joke between Paul Ince and myself. Just in case we won the league, we had some outrageous jackets on standby for the celebration. If we'd needed to win the Blackburn game there was no way that we would have worn them. The whole approach would have been more serious. But we'd won the league already, so out came the funny clobber. The competition was to see who could wear the loudest jacket. Paul's was pretty damn lurid, a fetching little check number, but I reckon I won hands down. After all, my

tie is even worse than Incey's, which surely tipped the scales in my direction. We got the gear from Phil Black, who had supplied the team with suits over the years. I told him it was for a bet, and asked for the most eye-bulging outfit he had. I believe he came up with the goods . . .

PAUL INCE:

Those jackets seem ridiculous now but you have to remember that we were both young at the time. Actually, I got even more stick than Giggsy because I was a little bit older than him. We thought we looked the part, but now I look back I'm not so sure, and it's not only my mates who take the mick – my children do, too. At all the clubs I've been to, as player and manager, people have brought up those jackets. It's something we'll never live down, but that's not a problem. We had just got a huge monkey off the club's back by winning the league for the first time in twenty-six years, and we wanted to celebrate. It was fantastic to be a part of that team and what made it extra special was that we were presented with the trophy in front of Sir Matt Busby.

" I'm a United fan, so to brandish that trophy once, let alone eleven times, amounted to pure euphoria. **"**

« Could I have dreamed I'd be holding the Premier League trophy so soon after getting into the first team? Absolutely not, especially after Leeds had just pipped us so devastatingly the season before. I felt every emotion possible – there was relief, excitement, happiness, contentment – it was complete fulfilment. I think you can see that on my face. There was this great outpouring of emotion all over the football-playing world, such is United's global support. But I could never have even fantasised that I'd still be there two decades later. Never! As a young player, you don't really think beyond the moment. The manager is different, no doubt plotting for the next year and the year after. I'm a United fan, so to brandish that trophy once, let alone eleven times, amounted to pure euphoria.

This would never happen now. It was September 1992 and we were in Moscow to face Torpedo in the second leg of a UEFA Cup tie. The manager said, 'Let's go for a stroll in Red Square', and so we did. One of the few photographers in evidence asked me to borrow this policeman's hat to pose in front of the magnificent St Basil's Cathedral and I was happy to oblige. We took the air, saw the sights and signed a few autographs. It was all very low-key and relaxed.

Such a sortie would be impossible these days because we would be besieged by fans and there would be absolute mayhem. On away trips now, if we're not training or travelling then we have no choice but to stay in the hotel. Looking back, I was lucky to have started in a less frantic era. As a first-time visitor to Moscow, it was tremendous to sample the atmosphere of Red Square. It's rather ironic that, as a wide-eyed teenager, I didn't take it all in. I would appreciate it much more now.

« It is the spring of 1993. I've been voted the Young Eagle of the Year at the end of only my second full season, Alex Ferguson is the Manager of the Year and we have travelled down to London to receive our awards. My jacket's not quite as loud as the one at the Blackburn match, but it's hardly quiet either. You might say I'd gone for it again, and this time I didn't have the excuse of a bet.

The manager looks so young. He might almost pass for my older brother, at a pinch! We took the train, and in those days we weren't really bothered by anyone. I was young and shy and I'd guess there weren't too many words exchanged. The relationship's changed now, obviously!

This was during the period in which the Gaffer was looking after me media-wise. In effect, he was protecting me, enabling me to enjoy my football with no outside distractions, nothing weighing on my mind. He was, and remains, a gigantic influence on my life.

SIR ALEX FERGUSON:

One day when we were playing Arsenal, George Graham came to my office for a cup of tea. I told him I had this fourteen-year-old boy who was certain to play for the first team. George asked his name, and I told him Ryan Wilson, which it was at the time. Then a few years later at another game, George asked me what had happened to that kid who was going to be a top player. I said he was playing today. George looked surprised and said he didn't see him. I said he'd changed his name and now he was known as Ryan Giggs. George's response? '******* hell!' He knew all about Ryan by then!

>> It was a huge privilege to be introduced to Nelson Mandela when we were in South Africa during the summer of 1993. I was staggered that he had heard of me, and even more so that he wanted to meet me. It turned out that he loved the game and was pretty knowledgeable about it. He told me he'd watched me and thought I was a good player. We didn't discuss anything of great weight, certainly not his remarkable experiences. I was only a young lad and pretty much overawed to be in his presence. It was only some time after I'd met him that I started to read about him and understand something of what he had been through.

As for the feller in the middle of the picture, Brian Kidd, he was one of the main reasons why I signed for United. Kiddo was the youth development officer at the time and I felt at home with him from the off. Once he even lent me his own boots. Nothing was ever too much trouble for him. When he became first-team coach he was a perfect link between the players and the manager. He was a lot more relaxed – you could raise things with him that you wouldn't necessarily want to mention to the Gaffer.

Kiddo always loved a joke. For instance, when we trained at the Cliff in Broughton, we would warm up with a few strides, then stop and stretch, probably over on the far side of the pitch. When Kiddo saw the manager approaching he would say, 'We'll be doing some stretches, then wait till he's almost here and then jog off.' So the Gaffer had walked the width of the pitch to see us, and then we'd be gone, leaving him to fume. There used to be quite a bit of swearing, but it was all good-humoured.

As for the training jackets, yes, they were disastrous, but at least we all had to wear them.

BRIAN KIDD:

People might say that I'm biased, and I am, but nobody can doubt that Ryan Giggs epitomises everything that is best about football, and the same goes for the lads that he grew up with at Manchester United. The way they have conducted themselves throughout their careers has been magnificent, and their legacy is nothing to do with the pounds they have earned but everything to do with what they have won and the spirit and togetherness they have brought to the game.

Ryan is second to none. Through all his glory he has remained the same humble, good-mannered lad, and he's a credit to himself and his family. It was fitting that he should be the one to break Bobby Charlton's appearance record, and he's right up there with all the icons and legends football has known. United gave him the platform, he responded and now he's part of the very fabric of the club. If I was able to help Ryan and the rest in any small way with my advice and support, then that has been my privilege.

» These boys in Soweto had nothing but their bubbling enthusiasm and their often breathtaking skill – and I'll never forget them. Some of them didn't have laces in their trainers, others didn't even have trainers but their passion for football was unmatched.

When we were in South Africa in 1993 we were given a day to do some coaching in the townships and when our bus rolled in to Soweto I didn't know what to expect. But immediately I was overwhelmed by the warmth of the welcome.

I was staggered by the boys' performance. They had me gasping in genuine admiration because some of them could do tricks with the ball just as well as any professional player. They had all the ability in the world, but never before had they been given the opportunity to display it.

It was an exciting day for me when I signed my first sponsorship contract with Reebok in the summer of 1993. Before that I had been with Puma for two years because the manager knew and trusted Martin Buchan, the former Manchester United captain, who was their Northwest representative at the time. Martin looked after me really well, but then it came to a point where a lot of money was starting to get involved. Various companies were trying to sign me, but when I met the man from Reebok I liked him instantly and the deal was done very quickly. They weren't big in football at that point; they wanted to make the change with me and I've been with them ever since.

« This was the press day at Old Trafford and there was a lot of posing for the cameras. I was covered from head to toe in Reebok products and all the attention was on me, but I don't recall being overawed. Everyone was really nice and that made it easy for me. I have to admit it was a thrill, all the kerfuffle, getting free trainers and tracksuits and gear. For a young lad, what was there not to like?

» What a cool dude! This was before the Charity Shield against Arsenal in 1993, when the players were strolling on the turf to get the feel of the stadium. This picture cropped up quite a few times in newspapers and magazines, but all the publicity, even if it was related to sunglasses rather than football, was never a bother to me. The media exposure didn't happen overnight but built up gradually, and I just grew used to it.

» This is a study in intense concentration, which is crucial to every ball-player, yet I can't stress often enough that everything good that I've done in the game has been purely instinctive. This applies in particular to the special moments in which, say, a mazy dribble or a perfect pass or a sudden shot comes to glorious fruition. That sort of thing can't be coached. It comes naturally as a reaction to any given situation.

So how difficult is it for a player to be aware of the bigger picture around him? It's something the manager preaches and I hope I've become more comfortable with it over the years. In my case, playing in central midfield and up front occasionally has helped me to appreciate team needs and evolve my overall game. For example, when I was at centre forward I'd know where I wanted the ball off the winger, so that when I went back to the flank I could be more accommodating in my turn.

⋁ If I'm looking dazed and confused on the Wembley grass, it's because United were enduring a hugely frustrating afternoon in the FA Cup semi-final against Oldham in the spring of 1994. A lot of our fans might have expected a bit of a cakewalk, but that proved to be far from the case as we fell behind in extra time. Oldham were a decent team who deserved immense credit for preventing us from playing well, and with a lead to hang on to they were incredibly difficult to crack. But just when it looked like it was all over for us, Mark Hughes scored a goal which only Sparky could have done, volleying in when he was off balance and under a heavy challenge. It was an unbelievable effort which changed not only that game, but the feel of our entire season. We had been getting tense as our Premiership lead was whittled away by Blackburn, but after Sparky's screamer we hardly looked back on the way to our first league and FA Cup double.

⌃ ≫ A lot of people have said kind things about my goal against Arsenal in the 1999 FA Cup semi-final replay at Villa Park, but as an example of pure, high-speed dribbling, my own favourite is this effort against Queens Park Rangers at Loftus Road in February 1994. We were leading 2–1 with about half an hour left when Ray Wilkins miscontrolled the ball and, having cut inside, I managed to touch it away from him before setting off for goal down the middle of the pitch. A succession of opponents, including Darren Peacock who is pictured here on the ground, approached me, but I was able to sway past them at full stretch while keeping the ball close to my feet. When I got near the keeper, Jan Stejskal, I just blasted it and I think he got a slight touch as it went past him into the net. In the end we won 3–2, so it counted as the winner, which made it even more satisfying. I always love playing at Loftus Road because it feels very intimate, with the fans close enough to the touchline for players to engage in an occasional bit of banter, and it always seems to me that United supporters take over half the stadium.

≪ Getting a handshake and a grin from Bryan Robson after I had scored with a free kick against Newcastle at Old Trafford in August 1993 felt like being presented with the crown jewels. Robbo was United's top man all through my boyhood years and I grew up loving him. Whatever I say about him, it won't do justice to my feelings about one of football's true greats.

He was a fabulous player and an inspirational leader who was brilliant to me right from the start. He would help me all the time, not just when I was flying, but when I had a bad game, too. If the manager had a go at me, Robbo would always be the one to sit by me on the coach, telling me not to worry. I would go from feeling utterly devastated to thinking, 'Well, it can't be that bad if Bryan Robson tells me so.' Sometimes it was just a passing word to two, such as, 'Chin up, don't listen to him.'

At the time Robbo was in his mid-thirties, but if he started a match I always felt we had nothing to worry about. If he came on as a sub when we were struggling I would feel better immediately. Just by a tackle or a pass, he could lift the whole team. He had that sort of aura.

He was a hugely generous character, too, setting me up with my business manager, Harry Swales, just when I needed him. Robbo was always thinking of his team-mates and how to look after them, being ready to fight their cases over contracts and bonuses. Football needs more men like Bryan Robson.

BRYAN ROBSON:

If I'm asked for an example for any youngster who wants to become a professional sportsman, then I have no hesitation in naming Ryan, who would have to come in as my favourite player of all time. When he started mixing with the first team as a fifteen-year-old you could see he was something special and that he would go all the way to the top. He never got carried away with all the hype, he just dedicated himself to his football and kept his feet on the ground, which is why he's had such a fantastic career.

At one time I tried to persuade him to play for England, who haven't had a settled left winger since the days of Chris Waddle and John Barnes, and he would have been a sensation. But he feels Welsh so he chose Wales, and I can't blame him for that. He's got a brilliant sense of humour, too, which is essential for any footballer. Ryan deserves every last bit of success that he has achieved.

» Did Incey and I rehearse this celebration, seen here after I had scored a late clincher in our 2–0 victory at Leeds on our way to the title in the spring of 1994? I must admit that we did. We were both young lads, especially me, and we were best mates off the pitch. I lived with Paul for a while and got on brilliantly both with him and his wife, Claire. Often we talked about what we would do if either of us scored – well, if *I* scored, because he hardly ever did! We wanted to do something special and we came up with this move on the training pitch. If I was to see that sort of nonsense from a young player now, I'd say, 'What are you doing? Just celebrate normally, what are you thinking of?' But I was still a kid at the time, quite naïve, and this seemed like a good idea. Incey was a great man to have in the team and I struck up an instant bond with him. We had the same sense of humour, but while I was quite shy, he was very outgoing, just the type I got on with.

As a footballer, Incey made a fabulous contribution, one that tends to be unfairly overlooked now by some United fans who were upset when he joined Liverpool. Certainly he was player of the year when we won the double in 1993/94. His energy was astonishing and he would grab games by the scruff

of the neck. He had this knack of hurling himself into a sliding tackle, then jumping up straight away and coming away with the ball, which gave us all a lift and drove us forward.

" I was a much better dancer than Giggsy! "

PAUL INCE:

We practised that celebration at home, in our bedrooms, in the front room, even in the kitchen, getting under the feet of my wife, Claire, as she was cooking. I think it was a really fine routine, nowhere near as bad as the jackets. When we did it at Leeds after Giggsy scored, everyone jumped on top of him; then when that was over we launched into our own celebration. To be honest, I think it only worked so well because I was a much better dancer than Giggsy! Great times, great memories, and I'll always think the world of him.

⌃ Champagne spray arcs through the Old Trafford sunlight as we celebrate our second successive title in May 1994 after a goalless draw with Coventry in the last match of the season. I didn't play because the manager rested one or two of us ahead of the FA Cup final against Chelsea. There was no way I was going to miss the championship revels so I changed into my gear for the presentation. Colin McKee, who can just be glimpsed behind Pally on the extreme left, took my place in the team, making what proved to be his only senior appearance for the club.

You can tell by the expressions that everyone is having a brilliant time, and no matter how much you win you never become blasé about such occasions, but I won't deny that this wasn't as emotional as the knees-up of a year earlier. Emerging from the title wilderness after twenty-six years, considerably longer than my lifetime at that point, was more than a little special.

≫ With his arms around our shoulders, a big, friendly grin on his face and the Premiership trophy safely in United's possession, the Gaffer is treating Lee Sharpe and me like a couple of favourite sons. But two years earlier, in 1992, with the title slipping from our grasp and the pair of us at Sharpie's place preparing for a night out in Stockport with our mates, the atmosphere wasn't quite so cordial when the manager came calling.

It has entered into club folklore how he received a tip-off about our intentions – it wasn't until a few years ago that I discovered his informant was my own mum – and charged into the house like a bull in a china shop, cuffing people out of the way as he went. He was red-faced with rage, like some uncontrollable force of nature, as he piled into Sharpie, who had been in a bit of trouble with him before. I was just told to go straight home and that he would be on the phone to my mum. I recall shaking as I drove back to our house, all thoughts of the Stockport outing forgotten, as were several United apprentices, who had been hiding in a wardrobe and were never discovered. After such an incident, the manager will never forget it. Not that he's one to bear a grudge . . .

SIR ALEX FERGUSON:

How did Ryan cope when I knocked on Lee Sharpe's door? I think he was scared! The smoke was coming out of my ears, and if anybody had stood up to me I would have hit them, I know that. I told Lee and Ryan that if they wanted to be my enemy, they'd find I was a very bad enemy. In the end they both had the same dressing-down and the same fine. Of course, Ryan was just a boy and Sharpie was also young at the time. But they had to learn . . .

LEE SHARPE:

The manager was really strict with us, and I always felt he thought I was the troublemaker because I was a bit older. Without going into details, I don't know if that was always the case! He was like a father figure to us, and I think there were pluses and minuses about the way he handled us, but nobody could argue with his results. In any case, usually the atmosphere in the dressing room was terrific. I recall one game when I was a sub, Ryan was playing, and I was filling him in about the defender he was going to face. Brucie had a big laugh about a nineteen-year-old passing on a few tips to a seventeen-year-old, and Alex Ferguson joined in the joke. There were occasions when the Gaffer could be very funny.

When Wembley's wet it's beautiful to me, and I've never known it wetter than that spring afternoon in 1994 when United were facing Chelsea with our first league and FA Cup double at stake. As I mentioned earlier, I wasn't a great fan of the old Wembley surface, which made it difficult to run with the ball, but this time the rain had made the pitch slick and I was able to really enjoy myself.

Although we were league champions already, we knew it was going to be a difficult game because Chelsea had become a bit of a bogey team, beating us twice in the league that season, with Gavin Peacock scoring the only goal both times. But now the gods were on our side as he hit the bar when it was 0–0 and we went on to score four. As soon as our first went in early in the second half – Eric slotting in from the spot after Denis Irwin had been upended – I felt there was no way we were going to lose, so I was able to relish the occasion.

Here I'm in a chase for the ball with Chelsea's Norwegian defender Erland Johnsen, and although my expression is grim and I'm utterly bedraggled, I'm loving every minute of it.

"The FA Cup has been won, the double is secure and all is well with the world for Eric and myself."

⌄ That day Eric captured most of the headlines, and deservedly so, after putting away his two penalties, both stroked perfectly into the same corner of Dmitri Kharine's net. The Frenchman didn't appear to have a nerve in his body; if he did, then certainly he didn't show it.

During the celebrations afterwards he was just one of the lads. He loved winning and he enjoyed a beer as much as any of us. He would never miss Robbo's 'team meetings', which might be described as marathon bonding sessions and which were often held at Mulligans bar near Manchester airport after an away match. The rule was that everybody had to stop by for at least one or two drinks. In practice some stayed, er, a little bit longer! After this game, though, we didn't wait to get back to Manchester, but adjourned to the team hotel in London. As for the bewigged Sharpie in the centre of the picture, I think he might have been looking for a mirror. No change there then . . .

CHAPTER FOUR

1994/95 1995/96

Another
double? Merci,
Monsieur . . .

>> I'm afraid my pleas fell on deaf ears when I urged referee Vic Callow not to book Eric Cantona one turbulent evening at Highbury in March 1994. I have to admit that Eric wasn't the best tackler in the world, but it seemed that whenever he mistimed a challenge, out would come the yellow card. He was a big lad and he looked clumsy when he tried to take the ball off an opponent, but unquestionably he was often penalised for offences other players got away with. In his case, it looked worse than it actually was.

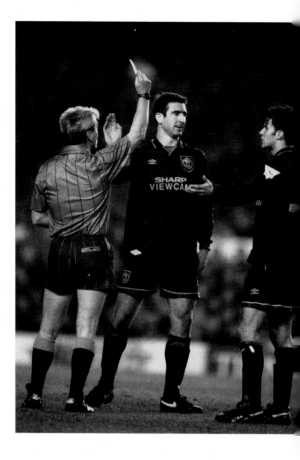

The fact is that Eric was 'The Man' and he tended to be targeted by opposition fans, which in turn could sway the officials. When Eric perceived that was going on, he didn't take it very well. You might even say he became a trifle irritated! He had this rebellious streak and he believed that referees and linesmen were against him. It can be seen here in the almost contemptuous wave of his hand. Sacré bleu!

>> Somehow it's hardly surprising that this almost absent-minded tug on my shirt by Crystal Palace's Gareth Southgate at Selhurst Park in January 1995 did not attract much attention. After all, it was on that chilly evening that Eric Cantona finally snapped, when he reacted to what was apparently a particularly obnoxious sample of poisonous abuse by launching instant kung-fu-style retribution on his wretched tormentor.

I don't really qualify as an eyewitness. I had seen him sent off and was talking to the referee and some of the other players when I caught a little blur of action out of the corner of my eye on the opposite side of the pitch. It wasn't until I got on the coach afterwards that I heard the police might be involved, and I didn't realise the enormity of it until I saw the incident on the TV news.

At first I was confident he'd return, even after all hell broke loose, but when he was suspended, even from practice matches, he began to get the hump and went back to France for a brief spell. Then I started to feel uncertain. The truth is, nobody knew his intentions. He trained with us throughout his ban, doing his community service straight afterwards. He seemed happy to be coaching local kids, and rolled with a little mick-taking from the lads. Mind, I must stress that it was very gentle mick-taking!

As for Gareth, his foul was out of character and completely without malice. He was always a very fair opponent and a really nice bloke.

≪ Manchester United players love the club blazer because it makes them feel so proud, and that holds true for me, too. The manager has always been a stickler for appearances at away games. He doesn't want to see us in tracksuits or other casual gear, and I agree with him. You are representing the club and I take the old-school view that we should all look smart together.

I hate to see players stroll from the coach, dressed any old how and with headphone wires trailing. Surely it's no hardship to take off your iPod for the minute it takes to walk from the coach to the dressing room? When opponents first catch sight of you, I believe you should look organised, like a team, like a unit ready for business, rather than a few mates on a day out. Occasionally the Gaffer might make an exception to the blazer rule if there's a really early start or a long flight, but that's different.

Down the years people like Sir Bobby Charlton, Wilf McGuinness and Albert Scanlon made it clear what a special moment it was when they were awarded their Manchester United blazer. It has always been something you didn't get lightly, a symbol of having reached a certain level – and it's an important part of club tradition.

This picture was taken at Ewood Park, Blackburn, in October 1994, and I'm wearing the same blazer that I was given as a youth team player of fifteen. I cherished it then and I cherish it now.

≫ Going through my pre-match warm-up routine back in 1995, the year I first had trouble with my hamstrings. After that they seemed to act up about twice a season. Usually I'd be fit again in about three weeks so it wasn't a massive problem compared to the injuries some players have suffered, but eventually the point came when I decided enough was enough.

It always seemed to happen when I was sprinting at my quickest, but I felt that it must be avoidable, that there must be a better way to manage it. So I tried weights, osteopaths, acupuncture, daily massages, daily back manipulation, iced baths, yoga – the lot. I've been very single-minded, exploring pretty much every avenue.

For the last three or four years I've been thinking this could be my last season so I need to make the most of it. It means extra work, maybe getting in an hour before the other players and staying at the training centre until about 2.30 p.m. I can understand some people thinking, 'Well, it's your job, you should be there,' and I'm certainly not complaining about my lot, even when everybody else goes home a couple of hours earlier. The bottom line is that I'm still playing in my thirty-seventh year and I still feel fit enough for at least another season, so I think my combination of treatments has paid off.

≫ There are not too many feelings in football which equal celebrating your team's goal against fierce rivals, which is what I'm doing here after Mark Hughes's header has flashed past Leeds keeper John Lukic during our 3–1 FA Cup victory at Old Trafford in February 1995.

When I first got into the team, Leeds were our toughest opponents – they pipped us to the league title in 1991/92. Then Eric arrived from Elland Road and the intensity of the feelings between the fans stepped up another notch until it was nothing short of ferocious. Every time he went back to Leeds with us the atmosphere might be described as electric, but to be blunt it was downright nasty. Distinctly unhealthy.

But I must admit I love to play at venues where the passion rages, like Elland Road or Anfield. It's a challenge and a very raw one. I never feel intimidated by the aggression, though when you're getting off the coach it can be a little hairy. I always thought it was a good idea to stay away from Eric at that point! They would be waiting for him, and they weren't about to make a polite enquiry after his wellbeing.

Looking out of the coach windows, sometimes you can see the naked hatred on the faces. Happily the majority have a healthy obsession with their team, but sometimes people step over the mark, such as making crude gestures and screaming obscenities even while they're holding their own children. Why do they have to do that? Maybe they're just trying to terrify the opposition, and I think that works with some teams. Not Manchester United, though.

» Chilling out in Volgograd in September 1995 with Peter Schmeichel, an extremely bright feller who might have been trying to introduce me to a bit of culture. On the other hand, maybe we were just posing for the camera!

On the pitch Pete seemed larger than life, an absolutely immense character and the best keeper in the world when he was in his pomp. He was a match-winner, no question. Even when an opposing attacker was through on goal with only Pete to beat, we never expected to concede. He was so big, and left his line so purposefully, that opponents could hardly see the target.

On some days in training, when he was really in the mood, he was unbeatable; we just couldn't get the ball past him. He would save our best shots and laugh as he plucked the ball out of the air. He was brilliant, too, at starting attacks with his throw-outs. As soon as I saw a cross go into his area I'd start running, confident that he would catch it and a split second be looking for me.

I'd have to say that he's the best I've known at United, although our current keeper, Edwin van der Sar, is very special, too. His hallmark is the composure he brings to the whole team, a quality which wasn't always associated with Pete.

Away from the game, our giant Dane wasn't quite as outgoing as he was on the pitch. Clearly a very decent bloke, he was usually fairly quiet, though you could never forget that he was a typical bonkers – or should I say eccentric – keeper.

The match in Volgograd was goalless, and we then went out of the UEFA Cup on away goals after a 2–2 draw at Old Trafford. But not before Pete had charged upfield to equalise a minute from the end, thus preserving our unbeaten European record on our own turf. He was some player.

» When the ball is there to be won, you have to go for it, even if the opponent steaming towards you is as fearsome as Neville Southall. This was in the 1995 FA Cup final against Everton, and I wasn't daft enough to entertain any delusion that he would go easy on me because I was a Welsh team-mate.

Neville was a wonderful keeper, similar to Schmeichel in that he was unbeatable on his day, and it was amazing how many times he saved Wales from getting an absolute hammering. But like most of the boys who make their living between the posts, he was mad – probably one of the maddest. Of course, I do mean that in an affectionate way, Big Nev, in case you're reading this!

Having lost out on the league title the week before, there was a real feeling of anticlimax about this game for United. I was still recovering from a torn hamstring, so I only appeared for the second half, by which time we were a goal behind. After five minutes I ripped it again, and although I was wearing a hamstring protector, the injury was both hurting and restricting me. Because it was the last game of the season, I played on, but I didn't make any great impact.

I don't mean to make excuses because Everton deserved their 1–0 win. But truly, if we'd won the league, I believe we'd have won the cup, too.

❯❯ This sums up the awful feeling of defeat on a big occasion. Until 1995 we'd won a trophy every season I'd been in the team, but this time we were losers and it showed. The expressions and the body language say it all. I was in pain because of my hamstring, which was stinging more keenly now the action had stopped and the adrenaline wasn't whizzing any more, but the real hurt was because we had lost.

I didn't want to go up and get my medal. I just wanted to get off the pitch as quickly as possible and go home. The Gaffer, standing there so disconsolately with his hands in his pockets, was pretty upbeat afterwards, telling us we'd had a great season, nearly defending the league and the cup, and that we'd be back stronger than ever the next year. Brian Kidd, in the background with folded arms, was great, too. He was tremendous at lifting us if we felt down. Oddly enough, that night was the best party we ever had, I can't really explain why, and the manager proved to be a decent tipster, too . . .

« It was 1 October 1995, the day Eric Cantona returned to action following the marathon suspension over his kung-fu antics at Selhurst Park. We were at home to Liverpool, naturally an occasion that had been hyped to high heaven. After an astonishing opening in which our inspirational Frenchman had laid on a goal for Nicky Butt in the second minute, we found ourselves 2–1 behind with about twenty minutes to go. Enter Eric, right on cue, playing the ball through for me to chase into the box. Jamie Redknapp tried to keep up with me, but I managed to stay just in front of him. Then he had a little tug at me and I fell headlong. It was a definite penalty. Step forward, yet again, Eric Cantona!

» There was only one outcome once we were awarded the penalty and Eric didn't disappoint, stroking the ball home with complete certainty before climbing the net-pole in celebration. Then he was engulfed by team-mates, including Phil Neville, who has him in a loose headlock, and David Beckham, who is waiting his turn for a cuddle.

When we started the season without our French talisman we were not downhearted. We knew we were a good team and thought that, if we hung in there until October, when Eric returned it would be like getting a fantastic new signing. We had a lot of young players coming through and had been written off in some quarters, but we never stopped having belief in ourselves.

Then Eric came back and got straight into his stride. There was an amazing series of 1–0 wins, with him scoring nearly every time, as we gradually reeled in the leaders, Newcastle, who had been a long way ahead. For Eric at this point, I believe everything about United was right: the way he was loved by the fans and the players, the way the Gaffer managed him, the responsibility he was given – it all fitted perfectly. He was a man in his prime in the right place at the right time. It is a rare occurrence.

" For any lad who grew up in Manchester with United in his heart, this would have been a magical moment, and I was no exception. "

« The place was Maine Road, the time was about twelve minutes from the end of a crucial local derby in April 1996 and I had just scored what proved to be the winner, putting us six points clear at the top of the Premiership table.

City had just equalised for the second time and the game was on a knife-edge when I cut in from the left wing and hit a rising shot through a little gap between goalkeeper Eike Immel and his near post. Somehow the net didn't really ripple, so it wasn't obvious to everybody in the ground that it was a goal, but I was certain so I set off to celebrate. Then suddenly I realised there was an eerie silence. Had I really scored? Had I been offside after all? It was a moment of horrible doubt when I didn't know what to do.

But finally it dawned on our supporters at the other end of the ground that we were back in front, our players came to give me a hug and I knew all was well with the world. It was a sickening blow for City, who were fighting to avoid the drop, but for us it was an enormous stride on the road to the title. Now I felt that the force was truly with us. We were on fire and we were going to be very hard to stop.

⍒ Some critics might not be surprised when I say we don't spend much time practising corners and other set-pieces at Manchester United. In fact, we tend to rely on the quality of our players to give decent service and to attack the right areas. Sometimes we might put in some extra work if we perceive a weakness, such as when we were facing Liverpool at Anfield around Easter time in 1997 and Gary Pallister scored with two headers from David Beckham corners.

Amazingly, Pally ended up being bollocked by the manager after that. At the end of the match the Gaffer had assured the press that we hadn't been doing any extra practice, but then Pally, who knew nothing of that interview, turned

up in front of the cameras to say we had been at it all week! It seemed the manager had intended to conceal our preparations from our next opponents, Borussia Dortmund, only for Pally to let the cat out of the bag.

I like to vary the delivery of my corners, sometimes opting for the far post, at others the near. Every now and then I'll just float one across; it all depends who we've got in the middle. Short corners can be pretty productive if the marking is slack, or maybe I might pull one back to Scholesy if he is free on the edge of the box. This one, against Spurs at Old Trafford in March 1996, didn't result in a goal, but Eric Cantona gave us a vital 1–0 win, topping off a run from the halfway line with a beautifully placed low drive.

⌃ Not quite getting in a tackle on Matt Le Tissier on the infamous grey-shirt day at Southampton in April 1996. When we came in three down at half-time, one of the lads complained that it was difficult to see each other against the background of the crowd, which was very close to the pitch at the Dell. In truth, the visibility was not the best, but I don't think we could blame the shirts for our predicament. It was just that we were playing badly.

Perhaps the manager had struggled to pick out players from the touchline, and he ordered us to change into a blue-and-white strip for the second period. We won that half 1–0 when I scored near the end, but that was no consolation at all.

Afterwards the players didn't say much about the grey-shirt business, and those who did mention it had a joke about it. But the Gaffer didn't think it was funny; he was deadly serious about the issue, and I guess he might have had a point. After all, if you're dribbling and your shirts are very bright, your team-mates stand out so that you barely need to look up to find them. But if you have to delay your pass for even a split second because it's harder to identify your target, then you're being hampered by something unnecessary. Then again, it might have been no more than an example of the Gaffer's psychology, blaming those dodgy shirts for the defeat – he is the supreme psychologist after all.

“A couple of people stopped and offered me money, so I had to explain to them what was going on. ”

⌄ I might be looking a bit fed up standing by this flower stall on the East Lancs Road back in the nineties, but actually I was having a terrific time. I was filming an ad for Reebok, one of a series which also included Peter Schmeichel and Dennis Bergkamp, and I definitely had the cushiest number of the three. Peter found himself on a pig farm and had to spend a whole morning up to his neck in mud and worse, while Bergkamp was sent to a cheese factory and did most of his filming inside a gigantic fridge. All I had to do was play with some daffodils for about an hour and I almost sold several bunches, too. A couple of people stopped and offered me money, so I had to explain to them what was going on. Daft, really, I could have made a few quid.

I was about 15, I think. My mum gave me the money to buy some new Reebok football boots. But on the way to the sports shop I decided to get a cheaper pair so I could take a girl to the pictures.

Ryan Giggs. Flower Seller. Cardiff, Wales.

DAFFS 75p BUNCH

THERE ARE OTHER BOOTS
BUT THEN THERE ARE OTHER CAREERS.

Reebok

⌃ This was the strike that put the 1995/96 Premiership title to bed, and it was a special day to me because it was the first time we had won the trophy on the pitch. I don't want to give the impression that the goal, against Middlesbrough at the Riverside, was especially crucial because we were already two up, thanks to David May and Andy Cole, and with only ten minutes to go I was feeling pretty relaxed. But then Butty played the ball to me and I just moved on to it, ran with it, then swerved a bit to wrong-foot a defender. I don't score many from outside the box, but I hit this one sweetly and it went in like an arrow.

⬐ For my celebration I did a little sidestep dance, but Keaney caught up with me and got me in a bear hug. He's looking happy, which might not tally with some people's perception of him, but actually he's one of the funniest blokes I've ever met. A lot of people have the wrong impression of Roy. They see him in certain situations on TV and they brand him in a particular way, but they're not seeing the full picture.

⅋ We had to put the effort in against Boro before the fun could start and here are Pally and myself at full stretch, doing our best to shut out Juninho. The Brazilian was blessed with fabulous natural talent and could damage any team if he was given just a little time and space.

Soon, though, it was party time, and nobody was happier than Pally, who really enjoyed winning the championship in front of his family and friends, and the folk who had cheered him on during his days as a Middlesbrough player.

« Just for a change, I was spruced up in my club blazer in time to face the cameras holding the most coveted prize in the English game.

⌃ Surrounded by the enemy – but somehow hanging on to both my balance and the ball – I'm doing my best to find a way to break the deadlock in the 1996 FA Cup final against Liverpool. I can't recall whether Phil Babb (6), Jamie Redknapp (centre) and John Scales came out on top in this challenge, but I do know that a fabulous late goal from our skipper, Eric Cantona, earned us the victory.

The game wasn't boring to play in, but for the fans it must have been an appalling spectacle, with hardly any scoring chances at either end. We were attempting to become the first club to win a second league and FA Cup double and Liverpool were trying to emerge as genuine challengers once again. That meant there was a vast amount at stake, so both sides played cagily. Under Roy Evans, Liverpool had some terrific players, the likes of Robbie Fowler, Stan Collymore and Steve McManaman, but somehow they never quite stepped up as a team.

>> We were all shocked when we walked out at Wembley for the 1996 FA Cup final and saw Liverpool in their white Armani suits. I'm asking Ian Rush, my Wales team-mate, if he picked them and he looks like he might be disowning all responsibility. 'No, Jamo, it was Jamo!' I think he was trying to change the subject,

and I can understand why. The stick they got for wearing those suits was enough to kill them.

It was great to have a bit of fun with Rushie, although it was no joke to meet him on the field. He was always a quiet person, but what an awesome goal-scorer! It was amazing to watch him train for Wales. Right foot, left foot, he would angle the ball into the goal, hitting the side of the net every time. Rushie has to go down as one of the all-time greats.

IAN RUSH:

David James and Jamie Redknapp were into Armani at the time, and they came up with the idea. They thought it was the in-thing and manager Roy Evans went along with it. But really the most important thing has got to be the football, and this simply wasn't the Liverpool way. If we'd won, the suits wouldn't have got so much attention, but Eric Cantona got a late winner for United and we attracted some criticism.

Ryan had a little joke about it, which was fair enough. During our chat we also agreed to swap shirts at the end of the game, which was my last for Liverpool. I always liked Ryan. He was a quiet, level-headed lad and a fantastic footballer. Being selfish, I wish he had been five years older, then we could have played together a lot more for Wales.

"Scholesy's a magical player who makes things happen."

≫ He might look like a cheeky young scamp as he sits beside me in the Wembley dressing room nursing the FA Cup after we have beaten Liverpool in 1996, but Paul Scholes was destined to mature into one of the finest footballers in the world. That day he was called on as a second-half substitute for Andy Cole, and he just picked up the pace of the game immediately. That sums him up for me. He works incredibly hard, yet everything he does seems to come so naturally.

Scholesy's a magical player who makes things happen. That's what he did all those years ago and that's what he's still doing in 2010. Actually, I always saw him as someone who would go the distance. Sometimes you can just gauge that when you train with a footballer. Even before he was in the first team, if he was on form then not one of the other players could get near him. In training he would come up against the likes of Keaney or Incey and he would just play passes round them. He would make it look so easy. And, crucially, he always had the temperament to step into a top side.

Basically Scholesy is just a very down-to-earth lad who loves his football. Ask anyone who has played with or against him – and I'm talking about some of the biggest names in the international game – and they will all talk about an unbelievable performer. This was the moment he savoured the first of his many honours, and it was a pleasure to be there with him.

PAUL SCHOLES:

I'm as pleased as punch to be sitting with Ryan, having a chat after winning the FA Cup. He was always a role model for me, as well as for Nicky, Gary, Phil and Becks. He was already up there, someone we were in awe of, and we all wanted to get as close as we could to his level. He was that special that he became a regular first-teamer when he was only seventeen, which gave us hope that one day we might achieve some of the things that he did. Ryan was always very helpful if you wanted to talk – that's if you were brave enough to talk to him, because he was already one of the best players in the world and therefore on a bit of a pedestal. He paved the way for other youngsters coming through by his fantastic example, and that hasn't changed even now.

CHAPTER FIVE

1996/97 1997/98

Win one,
lose one

>> It was the day Prince Charles visited Old Trafford, but I don't think David May got the memo. The manager, myself and David Beckham are all dressed up to the nines, and there's Maysie in his jeans. Now I'd like to stand up for my old team-mate, perhaps suggest that he filled in at the last moment when someone else dropped out, but no! You might say that's Maysie all over. To be fair, this is the smartest I've ever seen him.

The heir to the throne was at the ground for a Prince's Trust event at which we met a lot of youngsters, a really worthwhile occasion. It was the first time I had encountered him and I found him very friendly. He knew his stuff, was right up to date on how United were doing at the time and I think he was impressed by the feel of Old Trafford. I can't say he emerged as a United supporter, but we didn't have long with him so I can't be sure. We came straight to the ground after training, just in time for the pictures. I suppose that might be Maysie's excuse . . .

>> When the former Rolling Stone Bill Wyman opened a restaurant called Sticky Fingers, named after one of their most famous albums, in the centre of Manchester in November 1996, a few of the United lads were invited along and we had a tremendous time. Certainly Pally liked his food and probably saw it as a free meal. I expect he's a big Stones fan, too – that's his era really.

But what made it a truly unforgettable evening for me was when they brought round the vodka jellies. Kiddo, our assistant manager, didn't realise they were alcoholic. He thought they were just nice puddings, so he was downing them like there was no tomorrow, and after a bit he was the worse for wear. Butty and I – being comparatively sophisticated, obviously

– ripped him about that for a few weeks afterwards. Kiddo was a great mickey-taker himself, so whenever we had a chance to get back at him we jumped at it. He would have been in the picture along with me, Pally, Bill Wyman and Becks, but he probably couldn't stand up.

GARY PALLISTER:

Giggsy's spot on again – never look a gift horse in the mouth. It was a great night, and we all ate enough to put the place out of business. No wonder it didn't last long! He's got it wrong about the music, though. I'm far too young for the Stones . . .

BRIAN KIDD:

My memory of the night might be a little bit hazy (!), but I know we had a lot of fun. I have to admit I thought I was getting stuck into ordinary desserts, but I should have remembered that you have to keep your wits about you around Giggsy and Butty. They were just like Laurel and Hardy, though I'm not sure which was which.

" The frost was sharp, but it was a good night in Vienna. **"**

« We won 2–0 against Rapid to secure our place in the Champions League quarter-finals and I enjoyed a peach of a link-up with Eric Cantona. I managed to spin away from my marker near the halfway line and slipped the ball to Eric, who unleashed a real defence-splitter of a return pass which enabled me to side-foot past their keeper for our opening goal.

Eric was a prolific goal-scorer, but he took every bit as much pride in making chances as taking them. He was an extremely unselfish team player who never minded if he hadn't scored as long as the team had won. You can see the genuine enthusiasm on his face. He was like a boy, he just loved to play.

Of course, the magnificent specimen of manhood on the right is Pally, who had obviously been on the weights and was intent on flashing his muscles. I had swapped shirts, too, but there was no way I was going to remain topless at that freezing temperature.

» When Porto were the visitors for the first leg of a Champions League quarter-final in March 1997, Old Trafford was treated to one of its great European nights and I believe, with all due modesty, that I gave one of my best personal performances.

The Portuguese were very strong and we were expecting a really tough contest, but we beat them 4–0, playing some sparkling stuff in the process. That was us through. It doesn't happen very often that you can finish the job in the first leg, but that night everything came off. We lined up 4–3–3, with Becks, Ronny Johnsen and myself, playing a bit narrower than usual, in midfield, with Ole, Coley and Eric up front. People forget how excellent an all-rounder Ronny was. As a centre half he was up there with Jaap Stam, but he was tremendous in the middle of the park, too. A couple of times the Gaffer gave him the job of looking after Zinedine Zidane, and he did it well.

I just felt very good all evening and this is me shooting the third goal. Eric got the ball and delivered a beautiful pass to Coley as I made an overlapping run. Andy put me through and in it went from a tight angle, taking a bit of a deflection on the way. For me, that was the perfect way to top off a memorable occasion. Even David May popped up with a goal, the first. It's part of a centre half's job to chip in with an important one from time to time, and Maysie did just that.

⌃ Here's Lee Dixon on the seat of his pants which, if I'm absolutely honest, is exactly where I liked to see him. Unquestionably he was one of the most difficult opponents I ever had to face, but I always relished my confrontations with the Arsenal right back. I knew I had to be up for the challenge, right at the top of my game, otherwise I wouldn't be getting anywhere.

I seem to have skipped past him on this tense afternoon when the Gunners visited Old Trafford in November 1996. Of course, meetings with Arsene Wenger's team have always tended to be edgy affairs, but this one was particularly so because United had just suffered an excruciating run of three successive Premiership reverses, 5–0 to Newcastle, 6–3 to Southampton and 2–1 to Chelsea. I have to point out that injury kept me out of all those defeats, but I came back against the Gunners to help end the sequence with a 1–0 victory. In truth, it was a horribly scrappy contest decided by an own goal by Nigel Winterburn, but we weren't complaining.

« Some pictures have been included in this book just because I like them, and this is one of those. In this split second I am consumed by what I'm doing; nothing else exists for me but the bouncing ball. For some reason my left hand is tightly curled, as it tends to be in such moments. I don't know what that's about. I must do it naturally, sub-consciously trying to maintain balance while attempting to bring the elusive object under control. The shot was taken at White Hart Lane during the 1997/98 curtain raiser against Tottenham, Teddy Sheringham's first game for United, which we won 2–0 after he had missed a penalty.

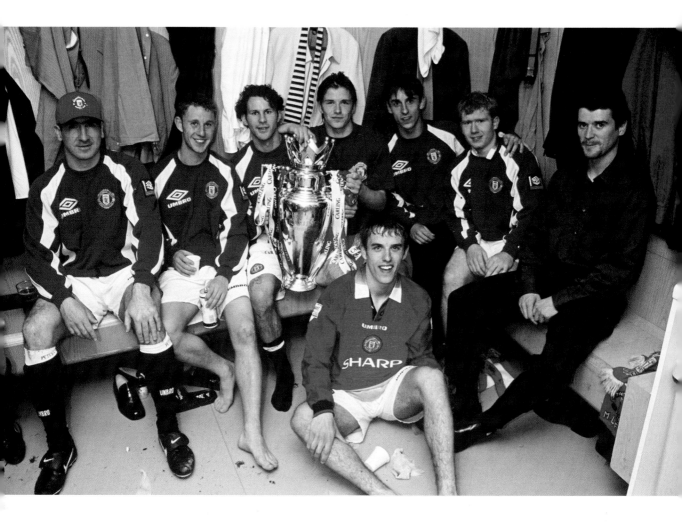

⌃ Sitting contentedly in the Old Trafford dressing room after being presented with the Premiership trophy at the end of our win over West Ham in May 1997, Nicky Butt, myself, David Beckham, Gary Neville, Paul Scholes and Phil Neville on the floor look a bit like a bunch of schoolboys with a teacher sitting at either end. Not that Keaney was that much older than the rest of us; it's just the dark expression he's wearing, probably a result of his having missed the game through injury, a situation which would have left him extremely frustrated.

At the time we didn't have the faintest idea that Eric had just played his last game for the club. He hadn't dropped a hint to any of us, although maybe, looking back, he hadn't always been quite as happy as in previous seasons.

Undoubtedly this new United generation learned a lot from playing with the great man, but I think it worked both ways. Initially Eric played in a ready-made team, with the likes of Bryan Robson, Mark Hughes, Steve Bruce and the rest. But then three key men – Incey, Andrei Kanchelskis and Hughesie – departed in the summer of 1995 and the team was revitalised by the boys who came through. I believe that process gave Eric new life, too, because he relished the atmosphere of youthful enthusiasm.

I'm sure Eric could have played on for another four or five years without any difficulty because he had a terrific physique. But he decided he wanted to go out at the top, and that's what he did. If his heart told him that, I'd say he did right to heed it.

⌐ Volleying a football is not an easy technique to master. The body is moving but the head should be as still as possible, a bit like a batsman playing a cricket stroke. When you connect, if possible keep the knee over the ball and strike through it. Co-ordination, timing and that old chestnut of mine, concentration, are all crucial because the ball comes at all angles; it doesn't usually just sit up nicely, so you have to twist and adjust in a split second. If you're even just slightly off key it will go badly wrong and make you look daft because a little tweak of the boot or the body can change the direction of the ball drastically. It could end up in the top corner of the net or the top row of the stand. Unless your name happens to be Mark Hughes, who was so brilliant at volleys that he could place them where he wanted them, you won't be aiming at a particular spot, just the goal in general. For we mere mortals, I reckon it's good enough just to hit the target and hope for the best.

⌃ If anyone wonders why I'm wearing an expression of utter amazement during United's 7–0 victory over Barnsley at Old Trafford in October 1997, it's because I've just scored a goal with my right foot. Believe it or not, I ran in from the left and just hit it as if it was the most natural thing in the world, and it flew into the net. No doubt Becks was just as astounded as me. In fact, I do practise with my right foot in training, though maybe not as much as I should have done over the years.

DAVID BECKHAM:

Yes, the surprise was there for all of us to see Giggsy's right foot leading to a goal. It's true he did work on it a lot in training, but it never changed the fact that it always looked like a swinger.

« It didn't happen too often, but every now and then we would know that the manager was concerned about a special player in the opposition. He would dwell on him at team talks, pointing up things he could do to unhinge the tightest defence, ways in which he could make a difference. Such a man was Gianfranco Zola.

Here, in United's 1997 Charity Shield meeting with Chelsea, I'm trying to shrug him off the ball, but it was no easy task. He was only small but he was deceptively strong, and he could create something where there seemed to be no danger, conjure up a goal out of nothing with a sudden backheel or a thumping shot. Like Eric or Scholesy he was very hard to track, drifting into positions in front of our defence, completely unpredictable and a constant handful.

But then, win or lose, after the game he'd always come to shake hands, invariably with a wide smile on his face. Gianfranco Zola – a great player who just happens to be a very nice bloke.

⌃ This was a big goal. It was October 1997 and we were leading at home to Juventus, who I thought were the benchmark at that time, the best team in Europe. We were 2–1 up and there was only a minute left on the clock, but we couldn't feel secure because the likes of Zidane and Del Piero were always liable to create a chance. Then Teddy Sheringham received the ball on the left, he slipped it to me as I ran inside him and as I evaded the defender Paolo Montero I hit it as hard as I could. In it went like a bullet, and although Zidane still managed to pull one back, we had won.

» Listening avidly to a word or two of wisdom from Sir Bobby Charlton ahead of the second leg of the Champions League quarter-final in Oporto in March 1997. Although he would never dream of interfering, his influence around the club is still enormous. His mere presence is such a boost, just for the calmness he projects. If we lose a game then he'll help us to get over it, put the defeat into perspective, tell us that we're a good team and that we'll win the next match. Even our foreign lads, who aren't familiar with all United's great players of the past, know exactly who Sir Bobby is. He transcends national boundaries and the players realise they are in the company of true greatness.

Back when I first came into the side, Sir Bobby used to join in with some of the training, especially the five-a-sides when we were on European trips. He must have been in his late fifties or early sixties, but with the ball at his feet his unbelievable quality still shone through. Right foot, left foot, fabulous balance, that little dip of the shoulder to send people the wrong way, his glorious ability was still intact. It was a privilege to see him in action, and somehow very moving, considering all he has been through with the club.

SIR BOBBY CHARLTON:

Ryan has always been a great listener with a superb attitude, unfailingly courteous and eager to learn, a professional to his fingertips. He's a terrific person, too, and you might call him a manager's dream, but that doesn't mean he's not as hard as nails when he has to be. Many's the time I've seen him step in to separate a few people when it's looked as if there might be fisticuffs in the offing. He hasn't lasted for twenty years at the top level without being tough.

But I can't believe where the years have gone. It seems only five minutes since I first saw him at Littleton Road on trials day, just gliding over the ground and going past player after player. Unquestionably he's made the most of his twenty seasons – and he's not finished yet.

∨ We didn't win anything as a team in 1997/98, which was extremely disappointing, but when the fans honoured me with their player of the year accolade it meant a great deal. I missed a few games that season because of my hamstring, which was frustrating, but overall I felt I was pretty consistent. Usually I operated from left midfield, but quite a few times I was off the frontman, so I was starting to vary my position. I was learning all the while, becoming a more complete player in the process, and I was delighted that the supporters appreciated it.

This is a beautiful trophy, mirroring the statue of Sir Matt Busby which stands outside Old Trafford. I love it because it's very imposing and so symbolic of all United stands for. Sir Matt was still seen regularly at the club when I was starting and, of course, I knew his history. He was a very old man by then, and not able to wield the influence, at least at board level, that Sir Bobby Charlton does today. But his very presence, his aura and his magnetism, were still intact. It's hard to explain, but there was something uplifting, almost magical about him that he never lost. Like Sir Bobby, he radiated calmness and assurance. When Sir Matt talked, you listened – and it inspired you.

≫ With his arm thrown around my shoulders, the Gaffer leads me away from the cameras and microphones. This shot, taken in May 1998, offers an apt illustration of the way he protected me in my early years at the club. I was by now usually dealing with the media myself, but he had looked after me brilliantly at a time when I really needed it. He just wanted me to concentrate on my football, knowing the pitfalls of being young and playing for a club like United. My natural philosophy was that if someone asked me a question then I'd answer it as honestly as I could. I was naïve and wasn't aware that they might be trying to catch me out, which can happen so easily when you're only seventeen or eighteen.

He showed me how to handle the occasional bad spell of form, and anything that might be thrown at me. I couldn't have had a better man on my side. I hadn't realised at that age that everybody wants a piece of you. Agents want to sign you up, journalists want a story, sponsors are after you, there are lots of people who just want to be your mate because you're becoming well known. It can all be overwhelming when just playing for United is pressure enough. The manager is an incredibly strong character and he wants the best for everybody connected with United. Maybe he'd seen a few not fulfil their potential earlier in his career, in Scotland, and he didn't want that happening with me and the other boys coming through at Old Trafford.

CHAPTER SIX

1998/99

The Promised
Land

⌃ We've had some crazy pictures taken over the years but this has got to be up there with the daftest of them. When a hotel was being built just around the corner from Old Trafford, Paul Scholes and I were roped in for a publicity shot, and what astonishes me most is how they got Scholesy to do it.

Do I often wait on him? Well, it's always me who gets him drinks in the pub, but this isn't quite what happens when we go away. I'm not quite so attentive. In the old days when I roomed with Incey I used to bring him a cup of tea in the mornings, but I've never done it for Paul. Mind, I do seem to be delivering service with a smile, while that might be more of a grimace on Scholesy's face. Actually, I think he might have made a bit more of an effort and put on his pyjamas . . .

PAUL SCHOLES:

It's nice, this, getting breakfast in bed from the best United player ever! I can't argue with that, can I? Probably he'd think it should be me serving him really. As for Ryan always getting me drinks in the pub . . . yeah, right!

⌐ What a way to spend a lovely sunny Sunday afternoon, being grappled by Martin Keown. In fact, nothing much went right for United that day at Highbury in September 1998. We lost 3–0 and understandably there was a certain amount of doom and gloom in the air among our fans as they trudged away from the ground. After all, Arsenal had just pipped us to the league and FA Cup double the previous season, then beaten us emphatically in the Charity Shield. There were question marks over our two expensive newcomers, Jaap Stam and Dwight Yorke, and now this. At such a low ebb, it would have been inconceivable to even dream that this was going to end up as our season of seasons.

As for Keown, he was always very tough to play against. On the pitch he was invariably aggressive, scowling, spitting nails, and he covered the ground at such a fearsome pace. Clearly this was somebody you'd never want to meet in a dark alley, an impression which was later underlined so vividly by his infamous reaction to a missed penalty by Ruud van Nistelrooy. But then you talk to our England players who got to know him and they say he's a great lad, amusing, civilised, exactly what you wouldn't expect after bumping into him on the field. I came to exactly the same conclusion when I met him at Soccer Aid, a UNICEF event at Old Trafford in June 2010. Funny game, football!

"Yorkie got away with talking to the Gaffer in a way that nobody else would have attempted."

» From the moment Dwight Yorke walked through the door at Old Trafford, he was a joy to have about the place. He was so funny, so relaxed, so good-natured, and he gave the dressing room a new lease of life. Such was his sunny disposition that he even got away with talking to the Gaffer in a way that nobody else would have attempted. He'd be saying, 'Come on, Boss, give us the day off. I've got to play golf, Boss!' Yet for all the laughs, such as this one as he celebrates a goal against Coventry in September 1998 with me and David Beckham, nobody could doubt that he was one tough cookie, both physically and mentally. Once he was in possession, he was just impossible to knock off the ball, and he was a strong-minded character. If Yorkie wanted to do something, then generally he did it.

During the summer before his arrival, the fans had been expecting United to sign one of the top stars in the world, maybe Gabriel Batistuta or Patrick Kluivert, and some of them might have been disappointed when the identity of our new striker was announced. But Yorkie changed their minds pretty rapidly, striking up a golden partnership with Andy Cole and bringing a new dimension to the team. Although we knew he was a decent player, we still expected most of our goals to come from Coley, but Dwight knocked in two in his second game and then never stopped.

As a winger, I was in wonderland to be playing alongside four such fabulous strikers as Coley, Yorkie, Ole Gunnar Solskjaer and Teddy Sheringham. I always had two targets; if the ball went forward we could be confident that it would stick, and all of them scored goals for fun. It was a dream quartet and any combination of the four was brilliant.

« No wonder I'm on my knees. United have just gone three down at home to Middlesbrough, we're off the pace in the title race and I can't understand where we're going wrong. As it would turn out, we were actually on the right track all along, because although we were beaten 3–2 in this game a week before Christmas 1998, we didn't lose another match for the rest of the season and finished up winning the treble.

In fact, although we could hardly have predicted the fantasy that was to unfold over the next few months, we knew we were playing well, so we weren't unduly upset. No matter what the results, if your game is flowing and you're creating chances, you know deep down that it's going to come good. And it did.

» When we faced Spurs at Old Trafford in the last league game of 1998/99 we needed three points to be sure of the title, and there wasn't one moment that we contemplated losing what amounted to the first of three cup finals in ten days. But, of course, we dismissed from our minds any notion that our visitors would roll over just because we were trying to pip their local rivals, Arsenal. That might be a fans thing, but players don't think like that at all. Professional footballers want to win every game they play as a matter of pride and integrity. Spurs were no different and they even took an early lead through Les Ferdinand, but we've gone behind plenty of times before fighting back to win, and that's exactly what we did here through great goals from Becks and Coley. My effort to add to the scoreline with this right-footer, despite the attentions of Justin Edinburgh (left) and John Scales, came to nothing, but that didn't matter in the end.

This was the first time we'd won the league at Old Trafford, and although we celebrated, there was not the same sort of abandon that there might have been in normal circumstances. We knew we had to go again, and again, very soon, and we were desperate to make history.

> **"**In the eyes of many this is the goal that defines my career. **"**

We were into the second half of extra-time in an FA Cup semi-final replay against Arsenal at Villa Park and, with the score at 1–1, we had our backs to the wall. Roy Keane had been sent off, Peter Schmeichel had taken a heavy knock and I was on the pitch as a sub for Jesper Blomqvist. The manager told me to play on the left but to get forward whenever I could. I started poorly, giving the ball away the first three or four times I got it, generally having a bit of a nightmare. So I decided that the next time I took possession I wasn't going to pass it, I was just going to dribble.

Patrick Vieira looked tired and I was lurking a little infield from the left wing when I saw him prepare to switch play. Hoping to intercept, I crept forward and the ball came to me. Then I started running with it, sometimes touching it, sometimes letting it run, doing body-swerves all the while. I seemed to beat everyone who appeared in front of me, and the next thing I know I'm in the box, where they couldn't touch me. Until then I wasn't sure exactly where I was because I'd been concentrating on the ball. Next I wriggled between Martin Keown and Lee Dixon, and then, as Tony Adams arrived with another challenge, I just put my boot through the ball as hard as I could. I was at a tight angle, running full tilt, so I felt I couldn't place it and didn't have the balance to side-foot it. I could hardly believe my eyes when I saw it hit the top of the net.

That was my cue to sprint off on a shirt-whirling celebration, but I was very quiet in the dressing room afterwards, even as I posed for the picture with Becks and Teddy, because with five minutes to go Dixon caught me

on my Achilles. I knew straight away that I had a problem, but I hobbled through the rest of the game and then missed the next six, including the trip to Juventus. So despite the high of the goal, there was the low of an inevitably looming absence. People often ask me if I'd been in control throughout my run, and the honest answer is 'Yes'. I wanted to keep going to see where it took me. Later I was amazed when I saw it on TV – I thought I'd received the ball about thirty yards out instead of inside my own half. It was a goal that came out of nowhere and it was a massive relief. That win gave us a tremendous belief that we could go on and win everything. And we did.

⌃ I've been involved in a few stunning comebacks in my time, but not many as sudden, or as satisfying, as this one against Liverpool at Old Trafford in the FA Cup in January 1999. Michael Owen put the visitors up early on, then we scored two very, very late goals to win. Manchester United just never give up. As we approached the dying minutes, still behind despite dominating the game, the Gaffer sent on Ole Gunnar for Denis Irwin and we threw everything at winning. Then, amid the most incredible atmosphere imaginable, Yorkie equalised and Ole poached the winner. To beat Liverpool in that manner, you could scarcely even dream it. When you're losing and then you win out of the blue like that, the emotion is overwhelming. So many feelings in such a short space of time – it can't be good for you but I'd never swap it.

This picture was taken during our last-ditch barrage, with Jamie Carragher (left) and Vegard Heggem combining to put me off. At that point we were not so much thinking about winning, as merely getting a goal to see where it took us. At Old Trafford, if we're losing with only a few minutes to go and we score, then I always believe we're going to get one more chance. So nothing is impossible . . .

⩔ I'm about to bite the Wembley turf after plunging over the knee of Newcastle's Rob Lee with Andy Griffin in close attendance during the 1999 FA Cup final. My eyes are still on the ball but it looks as if Lee's taken me out, so I'd guess I had to settle for a free kick.

We lost skipper Roy Keane early on after he received a bad kick. That was a particularly deep disappointment because we already knew Keaney wouldn't be playing in the Champions League final a few days later. The Gaffer's substitution was an incredibly positive one, though, bringing on Teddy, moving Ole to the right and putting Becks into the centre in Roy's place. Teddy scored almost straight away and we never really got to miss Keaney. For Becks it was a rehearsal for Barcelona, and Scholesy tied up the trophy with a goal shortly after the break. This was United's third league and FA Cup double in six seasons which, given the rarity of the double throughout the history of football, amounted to a remarkable achievement.

It's weird to reflect that we were playing in the FA Cup final at Wembley and yet it wasn't even the biggest thing on our minds. We had the small matter of a Wednesday night assignment in Barcelona to consider, so once again our celebrations were not exactly riotous.

" Butty and I grew up together in football and he remains my best mate in the game. "

» He likes a laugh, does Nicky Butt, one of the funniest people I've ever met. Everyone says how crazy he is and, years after he left United, people are still talking about his practical jokes and his wicked one-liners. Butty and I grew up together in football and he remains my best mate in the game, so it meant a hell of a lot to celebrate winning the league title together after beating Spurs at Old Trafford. We came through the same United youth side and he was the next to break into the first team after me, making his debut towards the end of 1992.

Butty was already a man as a teenager, exceptionally tough and intimidated by nothing. It was a massive tribute to his potential that the manager sold Paul Ince when he did in 1995, a move which upset a lot of supporters. Incey had done a brilliant job for several seasons but the Gaffer knew what the fans didn't – that Butty was coming through like an express train. In many ways Nicky was a similar type of performer to Incey. In his youth team days he shone as an attacking midfielder who got forward and scored goals, then later on he was more defensive, renowned for his abrasive tackling and sound positional play. Until Paul Scholes settled on his best position, Keaney and Butty were the regular central midfielders and we just felt so solid when they were performing in tandem.

NICKY BUTT:

I first met Giggsy when he was fourteen and I already knew him by reputation. The exploits of Ryan Wilson, as he was then, for Salford Boys were often reported in the *Manchester Football Pink*, and as he was seen as the local golden boy I expected him to be flash and cocky. In fact, nothing could have been further from the truth. He turned out to be a really unassuming lad, we just clicked and we've been pals ever since,

going on holiday together for the last fifteen years or so. Despite the incredible ability which shines out of him, he has remained very humble, and has stuck to the same friends he grew up with in the Worsley area. Had he wanted to project himself, he could have been the most famous footballer in the world, but that's just not him.

That said, Ryan is lucky in that he is widely perceived to be United's quiet man, but in reality he's always at the heart of the jokes and the mickey-taking in the changing room. If there's a wind-up going on, then it's a fair bet he is the culprit. If there's a party or a celebration, he is always the first one on stage with the mike, his speciality being 'Rapper's Delight', which he performed at my wedding. All credit to him, he was a bit drunk at the time, but he remembered the whole song, all seven minutes of it!

⌃ This is one of the most important goals I've ever scored, the late equaliser against Juventus at Old Trafford in the first leg of the Champions League semi-final in April 1999. As the minutes ticked away we were trailing to a strike by Antonio Conte, facing the grim prospect of having to come from behind in the Stadio Delle Alpi. It was always going to be tough, but this gave us something to bite on, a real boost. When you end a game on a high and the other team is therefore on a low, that can carry into the next encounter.

> **"** Playing for United for so long has taught me to believe that there is always the possibility of another chance. **"**

Late in the home match we were bombarding them and fashioning a few chances, but their keeper Angelo Peruzzi kept making tremendous saves. Teddy replaced Yorkie and stuck away a smart header after eighty-six minutes only for it to be disallowed for marginal offside. The situation didn't look good, but then inside the final minute Juventus failed to clear a cross from Becks and the ball dropped to me on the half-volley about four yards out. The goal-line was crowded with bodies, there weren't many places I could have put it and I could easily have sliced it, but I concentrated hard, caught it perfectly and it flew into the roof of the net.

In Turin we came back from the dead yet again, overturning a 2–0 deficit to win 3–2, so it's fair to say that my goal at Old Trafford was a crucial building block towards winning the competition.

» Even as I sprinted off for a mad celebration of the goal at Old Trafford, suddenly it occurred to me that there might still be time for a winner, so I turned on my heel and I was telling everybody to get on with it. Playing for United for so long has taught me to believe that there is always the possibility of another chance, an attitude that was to pay handsome dividends in Barcelona.

⩔ No prizes for guessing who is the only man grinning as United line up for the ritual team photo ahead of the Champions League final at the Nou Camp. Ten of us look tense and focused, while Yorkie is, well, Yorkie, appearing as laid-back as if he were readying himself for a kickabout in the park with his mates. Mind, he was every bit as professional as the rest of us; he just had a different way of showing it.

Certainly our two big centre halves, Jaap Stam (next to me) and Ronny Johnsen (next to him) are ready for the fray. The Gaffer had decided we were going with two wide men and two up front, which meant we might be exposed to swift counterattacks. So we needed a couple of central defenders who were quick and strong and solid, men we could rely on to handle one-on-one situations, and these two fitted the bill perfectly. It never worried them if we all went forward and left them with a man each, because not many could outrun them or knock them off the ball. Jaap got most of the publicity, perhaps because of his mountainous build and stern appearance, while Ronny tended to be a little underrated, but in my view they were as magnificent as one another.

The full line-up is, back row left to right: Peter Schmeichel, Dwight Yorke, Andy Cole, Ronny Johnsen, Jaap Stam, me. Front row: Jesper Blomqvist, Nicky Butt, David Beckham, Gary Neville, Denis Irwin.

⌃ The suspension of Paul Scholes and Roy Keane prompted the Gaffer to reshuffle the midfield for the Champions League final against Bayern Munich. He debated playing me in the middle, which would have allowed Becks to stay on the right, but he felt a central combination of Butty and Becks would give him a little more control. Therefore I ended up on the right, with Jesper Blomqvist taking my usual slot wide on the left. The personal change didn't bother me because I was used to being a right winger to accommodate Sharpie a few seasons earlier. I just wanted to play.

My immediate opponent was Michael Tarnat, an athletic left back who typified German efficiency and who would later spend a season in Manchester with City. Here I'm running at him while he is standing off a little bit, watchful for his chance to make a tackle.

≪ Despite our absentees, I was always confident that we had a strong enough team to beat Bayern, but their early goal knocked us out of our stride. It was always going to be tough after that against a big, strong, experienced side who were impeccably organised. Here it looks as if I've evaded the lunge of Stefan Effenberg (right), but the ball is squirting away and I'm about to feel the weight of a Tarnat tackle.

As the game went on we rode our luck as they hit the woodwork a couple of times, and Pete made some terrific saves. We didn't play particularly well but we stuck in there, and we won it in that breathtaking climax. In the end it was meant to be.

≫ The blessed moment when I knew the Champions League final had turned on its head. From being a goal down with the fourth official's three added minutes ticking away, suddenly we were level, and the sheer ecstasy on my face tells you how confident I was about the prospect of extra time. Our equaliser was no classic, but who cares? Becks took a corner on the right with the German defenders clearly bothered by the arrival in the box of Peter Schmeichel, who had charged forward because now there was nothing to lose. Over came the ball, Yorkie nodded it on and it fell to me on the edge of the area. It came quickly; I couldn't adjust my feet properly and I ended up dragging it with my right, which I sometimes call my wooden leg. It fell to Teddy and he turned it in from six yards, but I didn't celebrate straight away because I wondered if he was offside. Instead I jumped up to peer over at the linesman, then I saw him running back to the centre and suddenly I was claiming an assist.

Of course, there was fortune involved in the goal. We were lucky the ball reached me, lucky I shanked it, lucky Teddy was there, lucky he scuffed it. But there's nothing wrong with being lucky . . .

« My grin is threatening to split my face in two as I show the most precious prize in club football to our vast bank of partying fans in the Nou Camp stands. As a footballer, you want glorious moments like these to last forever, while the losing side just wants to go home.

» Paul Scholes looks happy enough, and I know he was genuinely overjoyed for his team-mates and the fans, but this was a truly poignant moment in the midst of the inevitable jubilation at the end of the final. It just didn't seem right to see Scholesy brandishing the European Cup in his suit, and the same went for Roy Keane, who was also there for the celebrations. It's hard to put myself in the shoes of these lads, two great players and friends who had been such a huge part of our campaign. To miss out must have been utterly devastating for both of them, although they didn't show that to us. I can't really grasp what they must have been going through as the action unfolded. All I can offer as consolation is that as far as everyone at the club is concerned, they were Champions League winners every bit as much as the lads who played that night.

PAUL SCHOLES:

It was a night of contrasting emotions, I guess. My main feeling was one of pleasure that the team had managed to win the biggest prize, but I suppose I wasn't full-on celebrating as if I'd played. Certainly, though, I was able to enjoy what the lads had done.

Ryan and the others made an effort to pull Roy and myself into the pictures. It was a little bit embarrassing, but they wanted the pair of us to be part of it. Both of us had played a few games on the way to Barcelona and it was disappointing to miss out, but that's just the way it goes.

CHAPTER SEVEN

1999/2000
2000/01 2001/02

Completing
a treasured
hat trick

> **"** I remember Giggsy
> rubbing my head
> in celebration. **"**

⌐ David Beckham always looked after his hair so meticulously that I was absolutely staggered, along with the rest of the world, on the day he revealed his shaven head for the first time. When he joined up with the team for the away game at Leicester in March 2000, he presented himself to the rest of us in all his bristly glory and the press boys on duty at Filbert Street that afternoon must have thought all their birthdays had come at once.

The cameras were clicking like crazy from the moment he stepped on to the pitch, but they reached an astonishing crescendo just after the half-hour mark when Becks put us in front with one of his classic free kicks. It's fair to say he realised he was the centre of attention as he debuted his new goal celebration with his arms flung wide.

To be fair, I think his new hairdo suited him, and certainly it set a trend, with lots of footballers through all the divisions suddenly appearing minus their topknot. Loads of people copied him whatever his hairdo – blond, streaky, long, you name it – and they might have been relieved by his latest choice because it was easy to mimic and to manage. I was never remotely tempted to follow suit, though, not after feeling how spiky it was when we celebrated the goal.

DAVID BECKHAM:

Giggsy and his hair . . . he was always moving it out of his eyes, pushing it behind his ears or putting gel on it. He's had a few styles in his time. It was my turn on this day – it was all cut off and a big surprise to everyone. Scoring a goal eased a lot of the pressure for me. I remember Giggsy rubbing my head in celebration and that being the main picture the next day. The person happiest about me cutting my hair was probably the Boss as I think he hated my floppy blond look.

« Old Trafford was packed to the rafters, the sun was shining brightly, we had just beaten Spurs in the last home game of 1999/2000 and the Premiership trophy was in my hands. What more could a man ask for?

⌄ Okay, I know it's a giant car key and not the Inter-Continental Cup, which United had just won by beating the Brazilian club, Palmeiras, in Tokyo in November 1999, but I was anxious to do the right thing by our hosts after being voted man of the match and then coming horribly close to putting my foot in it.

Straight after the game, when really my mind was still on the football, I was given the award and told that, for my prize, I could choose between a Toyota car or its value in money. Now, I had a car and, without thinking, my immediate reaction was: 'Oh, I'll have the money then.' But instantly I saw several people looking distinctly uncomfortable, so I did a rapid double-take and said, 'I'm only joking, of course I want the car.' That turned around what could have been a decidedly embarrassing situation, but it didn't stop me getting plenty of stick from the lads who, for some unfathomable reason, were much amused by the whole incident. To be honest, I was lucky to get the award anyway. I thought I played OK, but our goalkeeper Mark Bosnich probably deserved it more than me. And the car? I gave it to my brother, Rhodri.

⌃ Listening to Sir Alex in Rio during a break in our game with the Mexican club Necaxa, which finished one-all. He's a born communicator, invariably keeping his instructions clear and simple. As we have discovered countless times, a succinct word from the Gaffer can work wonders.

But it's a two-way street. He motivates us, but also we motivate him. If he sees that long-termers like Scholesy, Nev and myself have still got the hunger, then it strengthens his own. That shows itself in different ways. For example, we might be congratulating ourselves on getting a good result when we haven't played well – then he'll give us a sharp reminder that we're not going to win the title if we go on like that. On the other hand, occasionally when we lose he'll tell us we played well and that if we keep doing the right things then results will come. As I've said many times, Sir Alex Ferguson is a supreme psychologist.

≫ Taking a left-wing corner in the vast concrete bowl of the Maracana Stadium in Rio de Janeiro during our Fifa World Club Championship defeat by Vasco da Gama in January 2000. It was a wonderful experience to go to Brazil in the middle of our own season, but we weren't prepared for the unbelievable heat, which touched forty degrees at times. We did our best to avoid it by training in the shade at 8 a.m., but we were still shattered at the end of the session, when we would demolish huge watermelons because we were so dehydrated. It was just boiling, an alien environment a world away from the mud and frost of England in midwinter.

Not that we expected sympathy for going on what was widely decried as a mid-season break. In fact, we worked very hard on the trip and were disappointed not to do ourselves justice in the competition. True, when we knew we were out we had four or five days relaxing in the sun which did help to recharge the batteries, so we weren't complaining.

I'm glad I can say I've played in the Maracana, where you could feel the history although the fabric of the place was old and tired. There were drums, constant noise and dancing, which created quite a spectacle but the atmosphere wasn't intimidating because the fans were a long way back.

As for the controversy of missing out on playing in the FA Cup so that we could take part in the South American tournament, I won't pretend that the players were happy. We were the holders and we wanted to defend the trophy. Maybe the answer would have been to enter the competition using young players which, given the quality in depth at the club, might have been enough to see us into the next round while we were away.

⌃ Up and running for another new season, 2000/01, which ended gloriously, with United recording their first hat trick of league titles in successive campaigns. That was something we always wanted to do but which had narrowly eluded us before. Winning three on the trot is a mark of keeping our hunger, our desire to win things rather than resting on our laurels, a rare and precious quality which the manager possesses in abundance and which he inspires in his players.

"Does it feel fresh every time we win it? Yes, it does. "

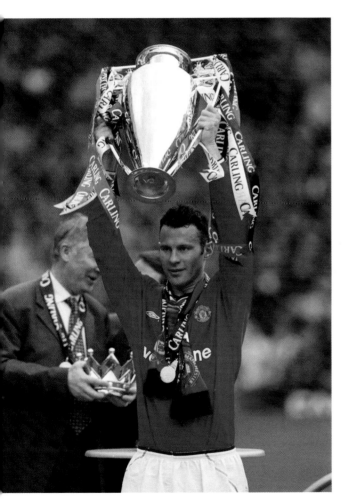

It was a funny sort of day at Old Trafford towards the end of 2000/01. The champagne flowed and the fireworks fizzed as we were presented with the Premiership trophy for the third season in succession, and the seventh time in nine attempts, but we had lost at home that day to Derby County. It was our final home game and we wanted to put on a show for the fans, but it never happened. At first, I guess, that dampened our spirits because we're all such competitive animals, but soon we began to look at the wider picture and we cheered up. After all, we *were* the champions.

Does it feel fresh every time we win it? Yes, it does. There's always a different scenario – it might be that we've played particularly well, or clawed back a big lead, or we hadn't won it the season before, or we've chalked up a hat trick. There's always something, it's always special, and there's always a certain relief that now we can enjoy our holidays.

The Gaffer tends to be ecstatic for about half an hour, then his mind turns inevitably to the future. I enjoy it a bit longer, but not too long. Probably the secret of winning so often is that we don't bask in the glory. Everyone at Manchester United understands that the most important trophy is always the next one.

>> If there are any harder taskmasters in football than Eric Harrison, I don't think I'd want to meet them. But the man who coached Manchester United's youth team for so many years, and nurtured all the lads clustered around him here at his book launch in 2001, was always impeccably fair to everybody who put in the required effort. As for the rest, woe betide them! Pictured here are Phil and Gary Neville, me, Becks, Butty and Wes Brown.

I first met Eric when I was twelve and it was instantly apparent to me that as well as being a scarily aggressive Yorkshireman, he knew his stuff. He made us work – didn't he just? – but he also made sure we played football the right way, so that it flowed in an entertaining fashion. Eric got the best out of us and I loved playing for him at the Cliff on Saturday mornings. His office overlooked the pitch and he'd watch us from there. If you weren't pulling your weight you could hear him banging on the window. I was on the wing so often I was the nearest to him and I can admit now that sometimes I would ignore him. If I did that and the banging stopped, he might have had enough, but more likely he was on his way down to give somebody a tongue-lashing, probably me. His creed was about dedication, attention to detail, doing the simple things well. Eric Harrison inspired fear, respect and, although it might not always have seemed the predominant emotion when he was in full cry, a lot of genuine affection.

GARY NEVILLE:

Ryan's right – Eric's influence was enormous. If Sir Alex was our father figure, then Eric was the grandfather. He instilled into us all the discipline, determination and spirit required of Manchester United players, while still allowing us freedom of expression. He's incredibly proud of what we've achieved and we all think the world of him.

⌄ Luckily for me, my testimonial match against Celtic in August 2001 was the first Old Trafford showcase for our two new marquee signings, Ruud van Nistelrooy and Juan Sebastian Veron, and the supporters were keen to see them in action. Ruud turned out to be a goal-scoring machine and soon became a hero, but sadly it never quite happened at United for Seba, despite his extraordinary natural talent. Possibly he was used to every move going through him, as it did when he played for Argentina, whereas at United we already had plenty of influential midfielders so the pattern was different and he never quite integrated.

The full line-up here is, back row left to right: Phil Neville, Roy Keane, Jaap Stam, Denis Irwin, Ruud van Nistelrooy, Seba Veron. Front row: Paul Scholes, David Beckham, Gary Neville, me with my sister Bethany, Fabien Barthez.

⋙ My sister Bethany was only nine when we strolled out at Old Trafford before my testimonial, and, despite the packed stands looming high above us on every side and the deafening noise from nearly 67,000 fans, she wasn't in the slightest bit overawed. She knew what it was like because she'd been coming to games from an early age and she took it all in her stride. She felt safe because she was with me, I never let her out of my sight, and she just enjoyed the experience.

At that age kids can go one of two ways. They can start crying because it's all too much for them, or they can embrace it. I see both reactions with the mascots who sometimes accompany us on to the field. There was one lad who asked me for the ball and when I gave it to him he ran off on his own towards the goal. His dad must have told him to make sure he scored in the Stretford End, and he didn't waste the opportunity.

⩔ There's a tradition of testimonial games between United and Celtic being feisty affairs and mine was no exception. Although we were coming to the end of our pre-season programme, our preparation was a little more relaxed than for a full-on game, but when the first whistle blew, the adrenaline cut in and we went at it hammer and tongs. Soon it became really fiery. Celtic had already started their season proper and were probably a little further on with their fitness, though I could still muster a gallop and managed to leave a couple of their players, including the current Norwich City boss Paul Lambert (left) on their behinds. They won 4–3, but for me, at least, it was a day to remember.

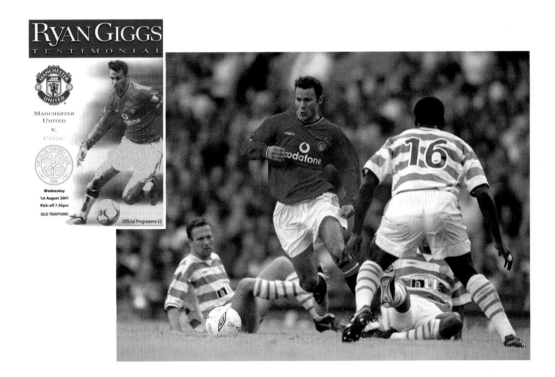

⌃ One of the occupational hazards of being a Manchester United footballer is getting drawn into daft pictures from time to time. I'm not too bothered about hamming it up for the camera; I see it as all part of the job, and sometimes it's fun. For some reason, the pictures tend to be a bit cheesier when the manager gets involved. When there's a big deal the sponsors always ask for Sir Alex, and he really throws himself into it. I can't deny that there have been some excruciating ones down the years. What are Ruud van Nistelrooy and I saying to our boss here? 'Pick us, or else!'

One looks cheerful while the other two clearly wish they were somewhere else as three United lads face the flashbulbs. Somehow it doesn't come as a shock that I'm the chirpy one, but how would you describe the expressions on the faces of Paul Scholes and Ole Gunnar Solskjaer? Sceptical? Embarrassed? Downright horrified? The club shares out the promotional work for sponsors but it was quite a coup to get this pair on the job because it really wasn't their thing. To be fair, Ole isn't as retiring as Paul, having grown much more comfortable with the public relations stuff as he grew older. How did they get Scholesy to agree? They must have offered him a free phone . . .

PAUL SCHOLES:

I think the look on my face says it all. Ryan seems the happiest of us which is not surprising because he just goes with the flow on this sort of thing. He's very easy-going, does what's needed to be done, though I don't think he'd do anything too ridiculous. It's funny, though, I don't recall a free phone . . .

⌃ Sometimes I'll look at a picture and it amazes me how I ever got into such a position. Even as I'm falling and shaping my body to minimise the impact, I'm keeping my eye on the ball and preparing myself to bounce up immediately to get back in the game. I've taken this tumble at Villa Park in August 2001, when it seemed very strange to be facing Peter Schmeichel. He was less than delighted by our last-minute equaliser, an Alpay own goal from my corner.

》 A typically dry aside from the skipper has got myself, John O'Shea and Roy Keane grinning as we stroll along the seafront at La Coruna ahead of our Champions League meeting with Deportivo in the spring of 2002. Keaney's wit was so quick that it was difficult to keep up with him at times. When it came to taking the mick he was up there with Butty, though their senses of humour were different. Keaney was very, very sharp, while often Butty was just plain daft.

As for young Sheasy, as he was at the time, he's a really easy-going, honest, wholesome lad, a solid person who has obviously had a good upbringing. He's a much underrated player, too, capable of putting in a shift in most positions and not letting the side down. When he and I played a run of games together in central midfield in 2005/06 after the squad

> ## " It's a wonderful thing about United that youngsters are accepted immediately as team-mates. "

had suffered a lot of injuries, I loved it and I think we complemented each other pretty well. More frequently, though, he has played behind me at left back, where he seems to do even better than on his natural right side. Sheasy's a tremendous all-round footballer, capable of nutmegging Luis Figo and of scoring a few goals, like that dainty chip at Highbury in 2005 that opened a lot of people's eyes about his capabilities.

Here, having just got into the team, it looks like he might be listening to the wisdom of his elders! It's a wonderful thing about United that youngsters are accepted immediately as team-mates. There are no cliques, no age barriers. I discovered that from day one.

JOHN O'SHEA:

You can tell I'm a new boy here, my trouser bottoms are pulled up that high! Keaney and Giggsy were always in huge demand from autograph hunters, so I knew I wouldn't get pestered if I walked behind them. In my opinion it looks as though Giggsy's said something smart, and is keeping his head down, letting somebody else take the blame.

Ryan's a fantastic personality around the club. He knows all the youngsters' names, makes everyone feel at home, but also knows how to bring people down a peg or two when necessary by having a quiet word at the right time. He's a perfect example to any footballer – how he lives his life, how he turns out in training every day, how he continues to perform so brilliantly at the highest level.

« This was the first thing I did for UNICEF, the United Nations children's fund, back in 2002 when they were launching a billboard campaign in Manchester, but I knew right from the start of the club's partnership with the agency that it wouldn't be my last. The striking image behind me represents the handprints and footprint of a nine-year-old Angolan boy who lost a leg when he stood on a landmine. As a parent, I find it hard to take in some of the gruesome stories about children who have been maimed by these evil devices, but when you hear the tragic details your heart goes out to the families involved. Landmines are a blight in current and former war zones around the world, and there are so many in existence that it seems impossible to remove them all, but we've got to do our best. The UNICEF people are doing a brilliant job on so many fronts – establishing orphanages, fighting HIV and sticking up for the rights of children in countless ways – and I will always do anything I can to help them.

» It will give me great pleasure to draw Edwin van der Sar's attention to this goal I scored against him when United met Fulham at Craven Cottage in December 2001. Edwin had left his line and miskicked a long through-pass from Scholesy, the ball dropped to me outside the box and I was able to thread it into the empty net. We won 3–2 and I scored another one, sliding in for a half-volley at the near post.

That day, I also discovered that Edwin wasn't just a magnificent goalkeeper; he was a passionate competitor and a strong character, too. He saw me moaning about something to the referee at half-time and he just walked over and pushed me out of the way. I thought, 'I can't mess with him, he's six foot ten!'

Edwin has been fabulous since he arrived at Old Trafford, definitely our most impressive keeper since Schmeichel. He is very composed, projecting a calmness that spreads throughout the team, and he's superb with his feet, no doubt a legacy of his total-football upbringing with Ajax. I wish we'd bought him straight after Peter left, but he went to Juventus instead, then on to Fulham, which was unexpected. Now he's having a glorious Indian summer at Old Trafford, and I was delighted to hear he's signed a contract that will keep him here into his forties.

⌃ Racing for the ball with Rio Ferdinand when we were on opposite sides of the great footballing divide which has always existed – as long as I can remember, anyway – between the Uniteds of Manchester and Leeds. Ask anybody at Old Trafford and they'll tell you that it's far preferable to play with the big feller rather than against him. I've had a few encounters with him down the years, first at West Ham where he impressed me as a remarkable natural athlete, and then at Leeds, where he stepped up a notch to become a truly immense all-round performer. Without being particularly physical, because that has never been his game, Rio was always tough to face, being quick and strong, an instinctive tackler and a brilliant reader of the ever-changing situations that football throws at you. It looks as if he might be beating me by a short head in this contest at Elland Road in October 2001. Happily, the only time I'm on the opposite side to Rio now is in training.

⋙ This is the autumn of 2002, soon after Rio arrived – you can tell by the hair, which was difficult to miss – and we are taking to the airwaves with Key 103 Radio for their Get The City United Day in aid of the hugely worthwhile Manchester Kids charity.

A stint in the studio was right up Rio's street. He's outgoing, loud, funny, a typical Cockney. In some ways he reminds me of Pally because he takes the mick out of anybody, including young lads just coming into the team, which makes them feel at home. He talks all the time. If you're wearing dodgy gear he's going to tell you, but more importantly he encourages everybody. Rio's a tremendous guy and he's great to have around.

CHAPTER EIGHT

2002/03

We've got our trophy back

⌃ Man at work. This shot captures for me the essence of what it means to be a footballer. I'm eager, totally absorbed in the play, intense concentration and determination etched on my face, my left hand clenched as usual. It looks like I've just changed direction at full speed; now I'm striding off my right foot while pushing the ball with the outside of my left. When you're being coached as a youngster they tell you to look at the ball, but when you're dribbling you need to raise your eyes to see where you're going and to assess the ever-changing situation around you. As a kid I found it difficult to play with my head up, but now it comes naturally.

The picture was taken during a 3–0 victory over Fulham at Old Trafford in March 2003. All three goals were supplied by Ruud van Nistelrooy, the most memorable of them the climax of a sensational run from halfway which would have had any coach drooling.

⌄ I never met a man who loved scoring goals more than Ruud van Nistelrooy, seen here celebrating after putting away one of his two penalties in the 4–0 home win over Liverpool in April 2003. Where does he rate among strikers at United in my time? Well, it's practically impossible to choose an order of precedence when I've been lucky enough to play with the likes of Sparky, Eric, Coley, Yorkie, Ole, Teddy, Cristiano and Wayne, but twist my arm and I'd have to say that if I wanted a chance to fall to someone in the ninetieth minute of any game that we had to win, it would be Ruud. He missed so rarely and he had every variety of finish in his armoury. He just came alive in the box and although he was well over six foot, he had really quick feet.

To me Ruud was a typical Dutchman: confident, strong-minded and technically excellent. He started scoring virtually from day one, which helped him settle. He got on well with the lads and the fans adored him. Was it true that if he had a good game but didn't find the net himself he wasn't happy? Yes. If we'd won 3–0 and he'd missed a decent chance, afterwards he'd sit in the corner of the dressing room looking miserable. We all accepted that, it didn't upset anyone; that was Ruud. If we were four up and he scored late on, we'd all be saying 'Thank God Ruud scored or he'd be sulking tonight.'

Once we beat Bolton 4–0, Ole scoring three and Ruud getting the fourth near the end. I made it for him and he ran over to me, hugging me as if it had been the only goal of the game and saying, 'Thank you, thank you.' Then he turned round to the fans and they'd all gone home. Well, not quite, but you know what I mean!

⌃ The glee on the faces of myself, Diego Forlan and Ole Gunnar Solskjaer, and the glum body language of Liverpool's Steven Gerrard, are more eloquent than any number of words in describing this Anfield scene on a sunlit Saturday morning in December 2002. Diego had just scored his second goal in the space of three minutes, a near-post snapshot after I had played him in, to put us two up in a game we eventually won 2–1. It was particularly crushing for our hosts because the first goal had been the result of a bizarre mistake by their keeper, Jerzy Dudek, who mishandled a gentle header back from Jamie Carragher, allowing our affable Uruguayan to roll the ball into the empty net.

If Diego never did anything else in his United career – and he did quite a lot, actually, despite getting off to a slow start – he would have been a cult hero anyway on the strength of this morning's work alone. As our supporters informed the world at the top of their voices, he made the Scousers cry. There's no better feeling in football for a United man than winning at Anfield. No matter how the teams are doing at the time, it's the toughest place to go. Emotions run so high, it's an old-school stadium with the crowd right on top of you and the atmosphere positively crackles. I know the rivalry between the fans oversteps the mark sometimes, but when United face Liverpool there's a special tingle and you know you're alive.

⌄ A joyous moment for me on two counts, as I angle my boot to direct a cross from David Beckham into the Liverpool net despite the attentions of Jamie Carragher during our 4–0 victory over Liverpool at Old Trafford in April 2003 on the way to regaining the league title. It made the game safe at 3–0 with about ten minutes left to play, and it was my first Premiership goal on our own turf for two years. You might say I was more than a little relieved.

⌃ This was the worst miss of my career to date, and immediately afterwards I wished the ground would open up and swallow me. United were going well in the 2003 FA Cup after big wins over Portsmouth and West Ham when we drew Arsenal at Old Trafford. I thought we looked the brighter of the two teams in the opening exchanges of a typically feisty encounter between the two clubs when suddenly my big chance materialised. David Beckham played a long ball which dropped over Martin Keown's head and into my path as I hared towards goal. I cut inside and managed to go round their keeper David Seaman, which took the ball on to my right foot. I wasn't sure exactly where I was, and as I was running I saw an Arsenal black sock so I thought I needed to hit it quickly and hard, which I did just at the moment I lost my balance slightly.

As I realised later, I could have rolled the ball gently into the net, but I went for power instead and it rose over the bar. It looked terrible, it was terrible, and I don't offer any excuses for it, except to say that bad misses happen to everyone at some time or another. Of course, it was magnified because it was against our main championship rivals, and they went on to win the FA Cup. Mind, it wasn't quite the main talking point after the game. That distinction was shared by the Gaffer, Becks and a certain flying football boot.

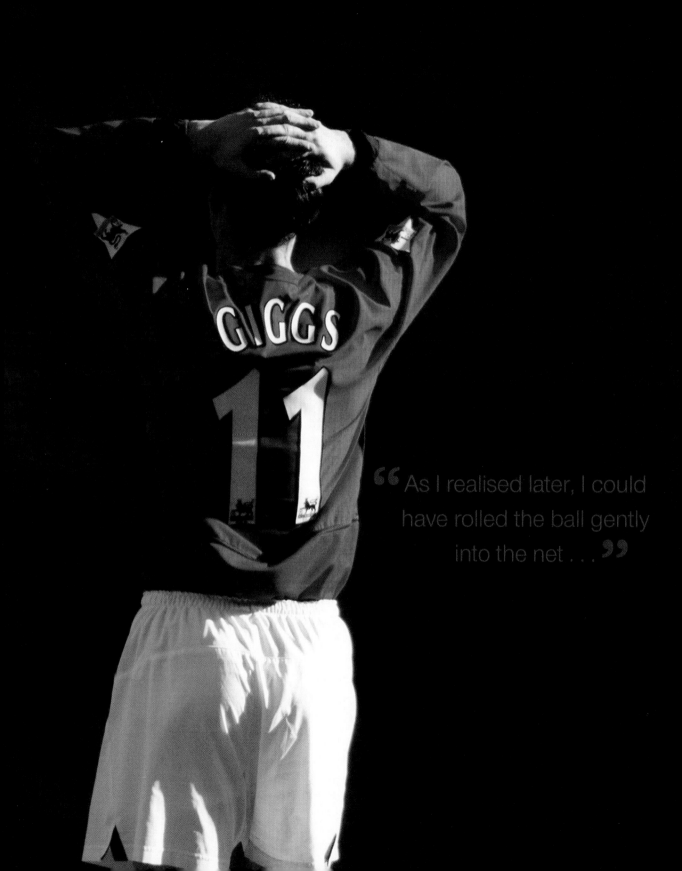

"As I realised later, I could have rolled the ball gently into the net . . . "

⌃ If we're talking Arsenal memories from 2002/03, I find this one from a couple of months later that spring to be a lot more appealing. Despite playing well enough to have been in front, we had just gone 2–1 down at Highbury to what looked like a blatantly offside effort from Thierry Henry. But only a minute later I had the chance to put us level, and this time I didn't mess up.

I remember my goal vividly because I didn't so much head it in as knock it in with my nose. I was playing off the front that night, so I was at the far post when Ole Solskjaer, who was in such good form that he was starting on the right ahead of Becks, whipped in a beautiful cross. The only problem was that the floodlights were situated along the stand roofs at Highbury and I lost the ball in the glare. I jumped to where I thought it was, but instead of me heading it properly, the ball smacked me in the face. Luckily it bounced the right way for me and we were level.

The body language here says it all. Arsenal's Freddie Ljungberg and keeper Stuart Taylor are a picture of despair at conceding so soon after scoring, whereas I'm well pumped up and Ruud is ready to push on for a winner. The game finished 2–2, which was a moral victory for United as we had been by far the better team. You could tell the manager thought the Premiership tide had turned in our favour when he went on the pitch to get the fans going at the end. After that we never looked back on the road to the title.

» If Laurent Blanc and I look a little like a kindly professor and his eager young(ish) student, that's really not very far off the mark. Laurent is an inspirational character, a cultured all-round footballer and a supreme professional whose enlightened outlook and freely given advice played a considerable part in extending my career. He set an impeccable example of how to prepare for games when you're in your thirties. For instance, he would come down to dinner on the night before a game, see what some of us were about to eat and say, 'No, no, you can't eat steak, it's too heavy. Have fish, have pasta, have fruit, have veg.'

He used to go to a detoxing clinic in Italy, run by a Frenchman, and I went there on Laurent's recommendation when I was suffering with my hamstrings in the early part of 2002/03. That went a long way towards sorting me out at the time and I'm still going strong eight years later.

When Laurent arrived at Old Trafford, he soon impressed me as a clever man and a clever player. He was very friendly, very helpful, but he was tough, too, as he proved on his United debut against Everton, when he was up against Duncan Ferguson and didn't give him a kick.

I really like Laurent, and it doesn't surprise me in the slightest that he made such an outstanding start as a manager at Bordeaux before taking over the French national side.

Our trip to play Juventus in February 2003 came at a peculiar time for me, something of a low point in my career when I'd been getting a bit of stick from some United fans. I hadn't scored at home for a couple of years in the league, there was that horrendous miss against Arsenal, and I'm told there were cheers when I was subbed in the League Cup semi-final against Blackburn, although I didn't notice that. It had never happened to me before but I think the criticism helped me, made me more determined, encouraged me to get back to basics.

Funnily enough, even before going to Turin, I think I was playing well again, and the thought that Juventus hadn't been beaten at home in Europe for a long time spurred me on. I was only a substitute, but I was called on early when Diego Forlan was injured and soon I had scored from a cross by Seba Veron. Then came the moment everyone remembers, when I sneaked up and intercepted a pass, kept running past a couple of

tackles, found myself in the box, then hit a shot with my right foot across the keeper Gianluigi Buffon into the far corner (shown here on page 152). This was one of my favourite goals for many reasons. There was the personal context, of course, but also it helped us to qualify for the last eight, Juventus were desperate to win, and I was being marked by top players such as Lilian Thuram and Paolo Montero. Definitely a decent night at the office.

⌃ I'm not exactly renowned for my ability in the air, but I like to think I've contributed my share of goals from headers, like this one against Maccabi Haifa at Old Trafford in September 2002. I've always had the knack of timing my runs into the box, and with the likes of Becks and Ole – or in this case Phil Neville – supplying the crosses from the opposite flank, I was always going to get a few opportunities. Usually I'm looking for a glancing contact as I make a diagonal run towards the crosser's near post. Often that's effective because it's a blind-side run and, if nothing else, it distracts defenders, which creates space for our other attackers.

❝You need to send out the firm signal that you're up for business.❞

« Caught in the moment of ultimate focus and controlled excitement before a big game, in this case United's Champions League quarter-final against Real Madrid at Old Trafford in April 2003. Sometimes you see players from other teams relaxed and joking at this time, but that wouldn't be for me. I think you need to send out the firm signal that you're up for business. What runs through my mind as the music is playing? I'm thinking about getting off to the best possible start, about my first touch, about who my direct opponent will be and what I know about him; all those things are whizzing around in my head. When we're at home it's important to get the crowd on their feet and behind us as quickly as possible. For me, that used to involve knocking the ball past my defender and then running him, but now I'm less of a conventional winger, so I'm more likely to consider drifting into the inside-left channel, maybe dragging a man with me. I want to find out how far he'll move to keep tabs on me, knowing that if he sticks close, it will create space for Patrice Evra or Wayne to utilise. Such are my thoughts in the minutes leading up to kick-off.

» Believe it or not, delivering this cross between the legs of Real Madrid's Roberto Carlos was a deliberate ploy rather than a miskick. It's something I often try if a defender is attempting to close me down and I haven't managed to beat him for speed. It's pretty certain that he will try to stop me from crossing by extending a foot, which gives me an opening. Maybe I shouldn't be giving away tricks of my trade before I retire – and at the time of writing, I hope that's not imminent – but I can't see how this snippet is going to help a full back's cause. After all, if he's to make any sort of block or challenge, he can hardly keep his legs together, can he?

This was the second leg of our quarter-final in 2003, when we were already 3–1 down from the first game. We always feel that if we can get a good start we can claw back virtually any deficit at Old Trafford, but this time Ronaldo – the Brazilian one – was on fire, and his hat trick made it a bridge too far. Still, we fought back to win 4–3 on the night and it was a hugely entertaining contest. To be brutally honest, though, that's not much consolation when you've lost.

《 This was David Beckham's last game for Manchester United, at Goodison Park in May 2003, and we're having a discussion about who would take a free kick. How would it have gone? Well, probably Becks said, 'Just stand there, Giggsy, I need a decoy.' Then, as happened so often down the years, he hit a beautiful shot into the top corner. Before he came on the scene it tended to be either Denis Irwin or myself in charge at set-pieces, but Becks's accuracy made him one of the best dead-ball merchants in the world, so I didn't have a problem with that. He was lethal from anything up to about thirty-five yards, while my range was not as extensive. We never had arguments about it, though once at Villa Park we both ran up and hit the ball at the same time. It could have been incredibly embarrassing but, although we didn't score, it did turn out to be a good effort, with the keeper having to make a decent save.

Becks and I grew up together as friends as well as team-mates, and we share countless glorious memories, so it was a shame to see him go. I know he went on to play for Real Madrid and AC Milan, and to sample life in the USA, but he's a United fan and I can't believe he found anything else to equal playing for United. Others have left to join some of the biggest clubs on the planet, only to find that the magic ingredient to be found at Old Trafford could never quite be captured elsewhere. Certainly I have no regrets about staying – I wouldn't swap my CV for anything else in the world.

DAVID BECKHAM:

I always wanted to take free kicks for United and, to be fair, Giggsy let me have most of them, but just that once at Villa Park we did get mixed up. We hit the ball at the same time and unbelievably it was on target.

We all shared amazing friendships over the years and I can honestly say my time at United could never be beaten for success, memories and friends. But I have no regrets, either, because I have gone on to play with some fabulous players and clubs elsewhere.

⌄ The ticker-tape explodes and Ruud van Nistelrooy brandishes the Premiership trophy after the presentation at Goodison Park. We won the game 2–1, through Becks's beautiful free kick and a contentious penalty from Ruud, though the title was already in the bag before the game. It was a fabulous moment in front of our travelling fans, particularly for lads who'd never won the championship with us before, the likes of Ruud, Fabien Barthez, Laurent Blanc and Seba Veron, and it was smashing that a few Everton supporters stayed behind to give us a cheer.

CHAPTER NINE

2003/04 2004/05 2005/06

A period of transition

❝ If there is pre-season training
in heaven, I reckon this is what
it might be like. **❞**

⌃ For the summer of 2005, United had the inspired idea of jetting us all off
to Vale do Lobo in Portugal for some fitness work ahead of the really heavy
stuff back at our training ground, Carrington. The weather was beautiful,
the atmosphere relaxed, the scenery to die for, we had our families with
us – it was absolutely brilliant.

If a professional footballer has a complete break of five or six weeks in the summer, it's going to be hell on earth when he goes back to work, so most of us keep up some sort of exercise regime, probably jogging on our own. That's what this trip was designed to replicate, a kind of structured but enjoyable prelude to pre-season training.

We'd start off each morning with a half-hour run on the golf course, which was closed for our benefit, then we'd do a few weights and a little bit of ball work on the pitch. After that it was back to our individual villas and the rest of the day was ours. In the evening there'd be a communal barbecue, which was terrific socially, and everyone seemed to love the set-up. Unfortunately it's not always easy to organise this type of expedition, what with so many of the players having World Cup or European Championship commitments, and we haven't been back since.

⌃ Upstaged by a gun-toting security guard – obviously a typically shy, retiring American – during our visit to the New York headquarters of UNICEF to meet United Nations secretary-general Kofi Annan in the summer of 2003. We were demonstrating a few skills to some kids when this fellow just walked over, asked for the ball and said he could do a bit of that – and he could! In fact, he was extremely nifty. I don't think the manager took his telephone number, though.

⌃ The turf flies as I let loose a full-blooded shot after cutting inside from the left wing at Newcastle in August 2003. I love playing at St James' Park because it's such an imposing stadium, the atmosphere is always bubbling, and we've had some terrific results up there. This time we won 2–1 courtesy of goals from Paul Scholes and Ruud van Nistelrooy, but my favourite trip was a few months earlier on the title run-in when we won 6–2. Scholesy scored a hat trick, Sheasy played a blinder – I got on the scoresheet when his shot came back off the bar – and it was my first game after my daughter, Libby, was born. Sweet memories.

≫ It's a funny thing, but most people seem to recall our 4–0 win over Bolton at Old Trafford in August 2003 as the game in which Cristiano Ronaldo made his United debut and brought the house down with his dazzling array of feints and stepovers. Somehow they don't remember this cool little dance routine that Keaney and I had been rehearsing for weeks in training.

In fact, I had just scored with a free kick, my first chance at one since the departure of Becks, so I was pretty excited, while Roy was usually the first on the scene for any celebration. Sir Alex has always insisted that we celebrate when we score a goal so as to share the joy with the fans. There were one or two occasions when that didn't happen and the manager had a right go. Certainly a knees-up came naturally to Keaney, which might surprise people who don't know him and are influenced by his often intimidating public image. He was the ultimate team player, a very open-hearted guy, and couldn't he just dance . . .

⌃ I can't help but cherish the memory of the only day (to date) on which I scored twice at Anfield, but if I'm honest I have to admit that I benefited from the bounce of the ball for the first goal. With Quinton Fortune lining up on the left, for a change I found myself on the right touchline, from where I launched what uncharitable observers chose later to describe as a cross. Whatever, the ball eluded the head of Ruud van Nistelrooy, for which it might or might not have been intended, then bounced up and sneaked in at the far post.

To be fair to myself, when you deliver that sort of ball you are playing the percentages, knowing there are various ways in which it might result in a goal. A left-footed inswinger from the right is a nightmare for any keeper to deal with, and so it proved for Jerzy Dudek on this Sunday afternoon in November 2003.

Not long afterwards I added my second (pictured here) from a narrow angle, the ball deflecting on to the crossbar before nestling in the net. Once again Lady Luck smiled and I wasn't going to argue with her. Liverpool hit back through Harry Kewell, but we took the points.

˅ Squirming away from the limpet-like attentions of Kolo Toure during our FA Cup semi-final victory over Arsenal at Villa Park in the spring of 2004. It was a tremendous game, a typically tight contest between the clubs and actually could have graced the Millennium Stadium as the final. The only goal came when I popped up on the right wing, received a lovely pass from Gary Neville and crossed for Scholesy to hammer home one of his bullets. Becks had just left and we didn't win the title that season, so the FA Cup was really important to us to keep things buzzing.

⟨⟨ After we beat Millwall 3–0 at the Millennium Stadium, there was an impromptu celebration in which the players took turns to dance around the trophy. I can't recall who got it going, but probably it was either Cristiano Ronaldo or Eric Djemba-Djemba (right), both exuberant characters. Sadly for Eric, he never built on the promising start he had made in the Community Shield, though that didn't surprise me after seeing him regularly in training. Some players find it difficult to adapt to the English game, and he was one of them.

After the final we changed into shirts bearing the name of Jimmy Davis, the young Manchester United forward who had been killed in a road accident on the eve of the season. Nothing could bring him back, but it was a fitting tribute to a nice lad and a good player who could certainly have made a living from the game. I don't know whose idea it was – probably Gary Nev's or Keaney's – but it was typical of United. It's a gigantic club but we still think of it as a family, and one which looks after its own.

You always remember your first major trophy and the FA Cup of 2004 was Darren Fletcher's. I was always confident that it wouldn't be his last, though, and so it has proved. He's picked up a handful of medals since then, and he's got massive power to add in the years ahead.

Fletch was unlucky in that he suffered a series of injuries when he was growing, then again when Becks left. Also, he was played on the right of midfield – he was never going to be a winger; he was a natural for the centre – and at first that made it difficult for him to be accepted by the fans. Some players will score an important goal and not play well for the rest of the season but still they'll be a folk hero. Others will put in one hundred per cent every moment they're on the pitch but won't get the credit they deserve. That was Fletch for a while. But I played against him in training, and I know when I'm facing a good player.

He's a really nice lad, too. He can be a bit fiery, but basically he's level-headed. He's made huge strides in the last couple of seasons, and is crucially important both to the present and the future of Manchester United.

⌃ A gentle jog in the Philadelphia sun with Manchester United's miracle man. I can use that description of Wes Brown without any hint of exaggeration because of his phenomenal record at bouncing back from a series of potentially career-ending injuries. He's done two cruciates and a lot more besides, yet amazingly he's come through it to win all the top prizes.

It seems to me that fans and journalists alike don't always take into account the enormity of what a footballer has endured. Sometimes they just seem to shrug off the lasting effects of major injuries, taking for granted the huge amount of time and effort needed to make a recovery, and Wes is a case in point.

Many years ago now, I recall going to our Littleton Road training ground to watch some fourteen-year-old trialists and I asked the coach, Eric Harrison, if any of them had a chance. He pointed to this tall lad with an unusual high-stepping run. It was Wes. He developed really quickly, and before long some of the wisest judges of a player had him down as the best natural defender in the country, adding that he would have been an England regular for a decade had it not been for his injuries. I agree with that, and it's testament to his level temperament that he just gets on with his job no matter what is thrown at him. He's a nice feller, too, a typical down-to-earth local lad who deserves everything he has got from the game.

This shot is from our pre-season trip to the States in 2004, when Wes was fighting back to full fitness after his latest setback.

≫ Is this my best side? I haven't got a clue why the photographer's gone for a close-up here during our Old Trafford meeting with West Bromwich Albion in May 2005. I might be about to take a corner and am staring into the middle distance to pick out a target.

⌃ I'm not the jealous type, but if it hadn't been for the fact that Wayne Rooney was on a hat trick on his debut against Fenerbahce at Old Trafford in September 2004, I'd have taken this free kick! 'You have it, Wazza,' I said, being the very model of generosity. So up stepped the new boy and curled the ball home as cool as you please, while his team-mates – left to right, David Bellion, Gary Neville, myself and Gabriel Heinze – stood and watched as if spellbound. There's no suggestion that we're poised to take advantage of any rebound; it was as if we all knew that here was a special player in a special moment, and there was no way he would do anything but score.

As debuts go it was stunning, with all three of his goals brilliantly dispatched, but now we know him better nothing could surprise us about Wayne Rooney. That night the gigantic expectations might have weighed heavily on his eighteen-year-old shoulders, but he made light of them with his fabulous performance, and he hasn't exactly let the side down since. He's similar to Scholesy in the instinctive way he plays and in his down-to-earth attitude. The arena and the opposition simply don't matter to either

of them. They are both incredible natural talents who are going to play their own way, no matter what. Whatever Wayne goes on to achieve, he deserves it all, because he's a great footballer and a smashing lad.

WAYNE ROONEY:

Giggsy has been an inspiration to me ever since I arrived at Old Trafford. He'd already been a superstar for such a long time, but what struck me about him was that he was still so humble and always ready to help. He's given me loads of advice on different things, such as what positions to take up, what runs to make and how to deal with referees. He's played alongside some pretty fierce characters in his time, people who might have approached officials differently, but Giggsy's way is the best. I'd call him quiet, but witty.

>> I'm not fond of flying and I get particularly nervous at take-off, so I tend to distract myself with a book. Usually I go for a sports autobiography – recent choices have included Ian Botham, Viv Richards and Gareth Edwards. This was the trip to Philadelphia and, as ever when we travel pre-season, we were on a luxurious plane with plenty of room to spread out. It's fair to say that professional footballers are pampered on long-haul journeys; we could certainly never complain about the way we're looked after when we're in the air. But I'll never enjoy it.

» I hope this goal made somebody's Christmas, coming as it did ten minutes into our home game with Bolton on Boxing Day 2004. Gaby Heinze crossed from the left, Cristiano Ronaldo flicked the ball on and it came to me awkwardly as I was running in. I managed to twist my body, helping it on with a kind of scoop that was part volley and part scissor-kick, and it sailed over the head of their keeper, Jussi Jaaskelainen, and safely under the crossbar. Scholesy made it 2–0 near the end and I was able to return briefly to my family before setting off for the next game.

What's it like to spend so much time away from my children at Christmas? Certainly it's hard to leave them to go training on Christmas morning when they've opened their presents and are enjoying themselves so much. In the past I never had a problem with being away at holiday times, but I have to admit that having kids changes your outlook. The bottom line, though, is that you have to be professional and accept that it's part of a job that does have plenty of compensations.

Rio and I might look like a couple of waifs clinging to each other for comfort as a storm rages around us, but actually the real story is a lot happier than that. The final whistle has just blown to confirm our 2–0 victory over Arsenal at Old Trafford in October 2004 and we are congratulating each other on an important mission accomplished. Rio is one of our most vocal players, one of the leaders who gets everybody else going. What's he saying? I'll go for: 'Hope the rain hasn't ruined my hairdo!'

» I'm coming over all artistic now. As I take this free kick at Villa Park not long before Christmas in 2005, the scene is illuminated by a shaft of winter sunshine and I couldn't resist finding a place for it in the book. It's a ground I've always liked. Villa tend to be a footballing team who go for it; there have been some marvellous games between us and usually we've gone home with a decent result. Also we've been involved in some terrific FA Cup semi-finals there, invariably coming out on top, which I guess goes a long way towards explaining my partiality for the place.

⌄ The brilliant Brazilian full-back Cafu of AC Milan, whose shirt I seem to have inadvertently grabbed, was one of the most challenging opponents I've ever faced. He wasn't renowned for his defensive capabilities, perhaps because he didn't have to defend that much, but he kept driving forward, forcing you back, and if you did manage to get ahead of him you would find the ever so slightly aggressive Rino Gattuso covering for him. With his remarkable ability to get up and down the pitch so quickly, you might call Cafu a second right winger more than a right back. This encounter took place at the San Siro in March 2005 in the Champions League knockout phase. Sadly Milan beat us 1–0 in both legs.

⌃ I enjoy every goal I score, but this one at home to Everton in December 2005 was particularly satisfying, partly because I managed to apply just the right touch to a dropping ball with the outside of my left foot to flick it past their keeper, but mainly because it offered a perfect example of the understanding between Paul Scholes and myself which, after all these years, now verges on telepathy. Scholesy was well outside the box with the ball at his feet but I knew what he would do and started running before he even played the pass. Duly he delivered it straight into my path and, having lost my marker, I was able to tuck it away first time.

These days Scholesy and I don't even need to look for each other. His awareness and his passing ability are simply sublime. He is a master of the art of playing with your head up, his total command of the ball enabling him to look away from it to assess his options. I'm a lucky boy to have played alongside him for so long.

⌄ They all count! I hit this free kick straight and true, driving it with all the power I could muster instead of clipping it, which is my usual method. In fact, it deflected wickedly off Benfica's defensive wall, horribly wrong-footing goalkeeper Jose Moreira before finishing up in the net. This put us in front against the Portuguese champions at Old Trafford in September 2005 and we managed to win 2–1. But it proved to be one of our more gruesome European campaigns as we were eliminated after losing in the Benfica return – the final match of the group stage.

« This trophy was particularly dear to my heart because it came from my team-mates at the end of 2005/06, a season in which I had extended my repertoire to include central midfield. It was the first time there had been a players' player award at the club, and although I had been pleased with my form over about a dozen consecutive games in tandem with John O'Shea after an injury crisis had enforced the reshuffle in the New Year, it didn't occur to me that I was in the running for this. At the presentation the Gaffer spoke of my game moving into a new dimension, commenting on how Sheasy and I had gelled together so effectively, and I had to agree with that bit of his flattery, at least. I can't remember who I voted for, only that I wasn't allowed to vote for myself, despite what some of the lads reckoned afterwards.

» Roy Keane never walked out on to the pitch at Old Trafford without doing his damnedest to finish on the winning side and, if the expression on his face is anything to go by, his testimonial between United and his new club, Celtic, in the spring of 2006 was no exception. Actually, he played one half for each team, and here he might be saying, 'Oh no, not Giggsy. I can't run past him. He's too quick.'

Ask any of the lads, and they'll say it was both a massive blow and an enormous surprise when he left halfway through that season. As a friend and a team-mate, he couldn't have ranked more highly with me. I'm not too sure about the circumstances of his departure; you can never tell with Keaney, and we never had a chance to try and talk him out of it at the time. If the impetus came from him I don't think we'd have had much luck with changing his mind anyway. We were all gutted, but now we just have to remember everything he did for the club. I'd say he was the most influential player in my time at Old Trafford, and when you consider the cast list, that's saying quite a bit. I caught Bryan Robson in the last couple of years of his career, but I saw the very best of Roy and, believe me, that was really something.

CHAPTER TEN

2006/07

Climbing back to the summit

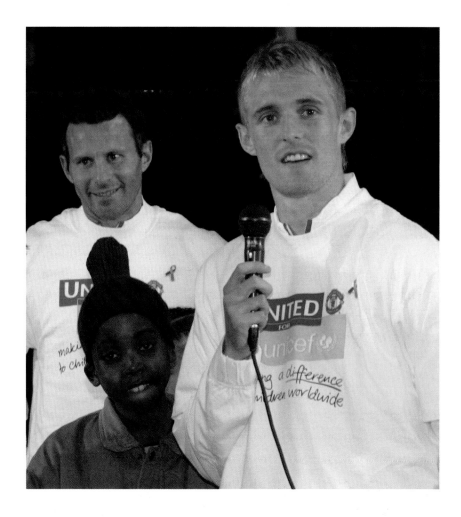

⌃ Put a microphone in Fletch's hand, stand back and just listen to him go. United were in South Africa in the summer of 2006 and called in at a UNICEF event at a Cape Town clinic for youngsters affected by Aids. There wasn't a large audience, but he emerged as quite an impressive public speaker, certainly far more confident than I would have been at his age. I suppose it befits someone who is his country's captain. The players are asked to do this sort of thing from time to time, and while some will always try to get out of it – naming no names, Mr Scholes – others are willing to step forward.

It was a privilege for Gary Neville, Wayne Rooney and myself to stand shoulder to shoulder with the man they call football's first superstar, the incomparable Billy Meredith, who played many hundreds of games for both Manchester United and City a very long time ago. Of course, it could only be a cardboard cut-out of the great man, which had been created in 2007 as part of the centenary celebrations of the Professional Footballers' Association, of which he was a founder member.

I've always felt some affinity for Billy because he was Welsh and a winger and he played for United, but there was an unimaginable difference between his lot as a professional in the Edwardian era and ours today. He must have been a strong individual to challenge the all-powerful football authorities of the time by fighting for better pay, and it's fitting that he's been honoured for his pioneering efforts. The history books say he was a wonderful player, too, and a hell of a character, renowned for running down the touchline with a toothpick in his mouth.

I'm happy to say that the union has flourished since Billy's day, and it is still doing a fantastic job for footballers, not so much for the likes of myself but for those who don't make the grade or who have their careers cut short through injury. I believe Billy would be proud of what the PFA has become, though goodness knows what he would think of modern wage levels. The shock would be enough to make him swallow that toothpick.

⌃ A moment of despair so black that I couldn't even think about the penalty I'd just gained after being pulled down by keeper Artur Boruc in the Champions League clash with Celtic at Old Trafford in September 2006. I sprinted on to a long ball, he caught me as I knocked it past him at speed and my hamstring has gone. I got stick from the Celtic fans for what they thought was a dive, but it was absolutely genuine. I was pushing myself to twist round Boruc at speed, my back and my hamstring were pulling in different directions and my body couldn't take the pressure. I knew in that instant as I lay on my back grimacing with pain that my old injury had recurred, that I was facing weeks of rehabilitation and would miss a minimum of four or five games. Of course, I've been much more fortunate than many players who have faced far more serious injuries, and for that I thank my lucky stars, but that wasn't uppermost in my mind as I limped off.

I've investigated every way of avoiding the problem, such as yoga, and it has helped that as I've got older I've slowed down a bit, so I'm not taking my body to such extremes. As I prepare so thoroughly, at least I can be certain that the injury has never recurred through carelessness, or because I hadn't warmed up properly or had allowed myself to become tired ahead of a game.

By the way, Louis Saha converted the penalty and we went on to win 3–2.

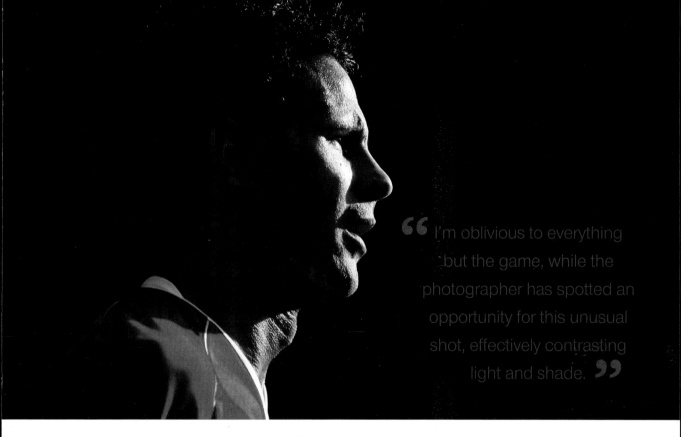

" I'm oblivious to everything but the game, while the photographer has spotted an opportunity for this unusual shot, effectively contrasting light and shade. "

« What you might call a candid snap, when I had no idea that the cameraman was about to press the button. Do I get fed up with being pictured from every angle, no matter what I'm doing, all at the whim of somebody else? In football surroundings – and this was at a press conference – I don't mind. I've grown used to it. But away from the game, I don't like it. I'll never become accustomed to walking down the road and having the paparazzi snatch a photograph. I can't get my head round that, it doesn't feel normal and I don't know how to react. It's intrusive and it's wrong, but that's just the way it is, part of everyday life for a professional footballer.

⌃ What's the Gaffer said in this press conference that has left me looking so perplexed? Probably he's just announced the team and I'm not in it! The players take it in turns to make appearances with him, before Champions League games and for various sponsorship deals and launches. Sir Alex is a very impressive performer on such occasions, handling most things that can be thrown at him exceptionally well. Even when he has a major speech to make, perhaps at a dinner, he just reels it off without referring to any notes. Considering that he does so many, and that you hardly ever hear him repeat himself, it's amazing.

» In the company of heroes. Gary Neville, Bryan Robson, Sir Alex, Steve Bruce, myself and Peter Schmeichel raise a glass to celebrate the Gaffer's staggering longevity with Manchester United. His achievements in the game have been colossal, and his players down the years have learned so much from him. It's no wonder that so many of his charges come to him for advice, and that he's held in universal esteem. Whatever I do when I stop playing – and I have no idea what that will be – I'll always remember the lessons he taught me as a lad growing up, about how to conduct myself on and off the pitch and the true meaning of respect.

> **"** I'll always remember the lessons he taught me as a lad growing up. **"**

When we gathered to honour the manager, it was marvellous to be reunited with some of the men who were already top performers when I broke into the team. Brucie, for one, was a massive influence on me. He was always so much fun, so bubbly, but what a warrior, too.

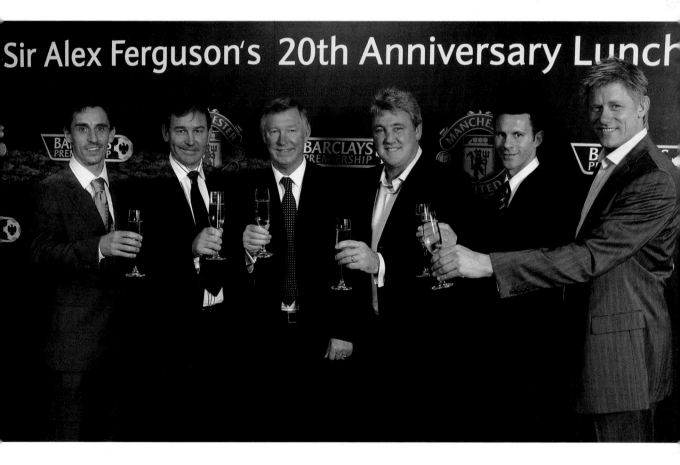

« You see, I do use my right foot for more than standing on! Somehow it looks a little weird when left-footers hit the ball with their right, because in general they're so much associated with their stronger leg, more reliant on it than their right-sided counterparts. In fairness to myself, I think I'm OK with my right – I can cross at full speed and have even scored the occasional goal with my so-called swinger. The manager complimented me on that quite early in my career, although maybe he was just buttering me up to play on the right wing when Lee Sharpe was at the club. Later on, I used to switch wings with Cristiano every now and again. Sometimes I even surprise an opponent by doing something half-decent with my right foot.

» Everyone loves Ole Gunnar Solskjaer. He's a great person as well as a wonderful footballer, and we were all delighted for him during that magical spell during 2006/07 when he returned from his long injury lay-off and started scoring goals as if he'd never been away. This one came at Wigan in the autumn and it was an opportunity for some of the newer lads, like Michael Carrick and Nemanja Vidic in the picture, to appreciate what all the fuss was about where Ole was concerned. Previously they had heard about him and seen him in the gym, but this was the real McCoy.

The first time I encountered Ole in training it blew me away. I went home and told my mates I had just seen the new Alan Shearer. His technique was incredible and I couldn't believe that it was possible for anyone to be so consistently accurate. He could score every sort of goal, left-foot, right-foot, headers, volleys, nudges, they all seemed to go in, usually hitting the inside of the net low and hard. I'm not surprised that he's gone into coaching at United because he loves the game so much. He's a clever bloke, very determined, and he's made a tremendous start with the reserves. I can see him becoming a top manager one day.

OLE GUNNAR SOLSKJAER:

I am nine months older than Ryan but he was already a star for Manchester United at seventeen, an age at which I was nowhere near the first team of my local club in Norway. Since then I've come to Old Trafford, gone through my whole career and been retired for three years, yet Ryan is still going strong. He is absolutely remarkable. When I arrived I felt like a little kid in his presence, but he was very friendly and put me at my ease. These days, if I ask him to have a word with the young players he is always willing, there is never a 'no' in his mouth. I'm proud to tell my kids that I played with Ryan Giggs, even though I did my best to wriggle away from him during this goal celebration at Wigan.

⌃ This was a deeply satisfying and much-needed goal which some people assumed wrongly to be a miskick. We were trailing 1–0 to Fulham at Craven Cottage in February 2007 when Wayne Rooney delivered the ball in the air to the right side of the box, where I had drifted away from my marker. I wanted to direct it back across the keeper, Jan Lastuvka, and because of the angle it had arrived the only way I could do that was to cut my foot across the ball. It was quite a delicate touch, actually, not easy to execute, and it was ironic that some people thought I had shinned it.

" The afternoon got even better for us as Cristiano Ronaldo scored a typically brilliant late winner. "

Same match, but different body language! Every game has its ups and downs. Although it's always a tough contest at the Cottage, and we've had some poor results there in recent seasons, I enjoy our visits there. It's an old-school ground with the crowd right on top of you, and we always have magnificent support behind one of the goals.

⌃ Considering that the opposing team walked off the pitch in protest, it's fair to say that this is the most controversial goal I've ever scored. We were in Lille for the opening game of the Champions League knockout stage in February 2007 and, with only seven or eight minutes to go, it had been a very tight contest with no goals. Then Louis Saha was fouled and we got a free kick just outside the box. As they started lining up their wall, Wayne Rooney had the ball in his hands and I asked the referee if we could take it straight away. He said 'yes' and blew his whistle, so I told Wayne to put it down quickly. He did and I curled it through a gap into their empty net.

I realised they weren't ready because their keeper was out with his defenders, but that was up to him. Certainly it caused a hell of a fuss, and they even walked off at one point, but I was amazed that their reaction was quite so heated. Maybe in France the custom is different, but if you see an opportunity you have to take it. Certainly I had no regrets about scoring what proved to be the winner in the way I did. How upset were they? Well, when the game resumed I wasn't exactly their favourite person, but that was like water off a duck's back to me. As for Wayne, he caught on really quickly – later he claimed an assist!

⌐ Although there's no getting away from the fact that Kaka has grabbed me by the throat, I'm happy to say that this confrontation with AC Milan's Brazilian star was nowhere near as serious as it looked. During the first leg of our Champions League semi-final at Old Trafford in 2007, one of our lads had fouled him, he'd urged the referee to book the offender, and I went over to say, 'You don't do that.' That's when he took hold of me, and when I realised how big he was.

In truth, it was only a light hand. There was no way he was throttling me in anger or I probably wouldn't be here to tell the story. Before the second leg he showed there was no malice by approaching me with a smile on his face and jokingly raising his hand to my neck. Things can happen in the heat of the moment, and in his culture getting people booked might be acceptable, while in ours it isn't.

⌃ That big grin on the face of Cristiano as we rejoice over his goal in our 3–1 win over City at Old Trafford in December 2006 sums up his personality perfectly. He was always a cheerful soul around the place, a brilliant presence in the dressing room, especially when he was treating us to his very funny impressions of various team-mates. He was a popular lad and, football considerations to one side, we miss him as a character.

I used to change next to him; we chatted a lot and I got to know him well. As a player, when he came to Manchester he was very raw but he was always confident, with a deep inner belief and the skills to back it up. He made huge waves with his showboating debut against Bolton, which was hugely entertaining for the fans but it became a bit of a millstone round his neck because it is impossible to reproduce that sort of performance in every game.

As Cristiano developed into the best footballer in the world, he gave our team a different dimension, and he earned every bit of the acclamation that went his way. He lived his life in the right way, working hard, practising conscientiously, eating well. He was kicked all over the place by defenders, but it didn't bother him; he just wanted the ball. More recently his game has matured; he has become more of a passer, while the inclination to dive has become less and less noticeable. As for his shooting, his heading, his speed and his strength, well, he's not too shabby a player, is he?

⋙ Cristiano liked to have fun and our head-tennis routines at Carrington offered an ideal outlet for him. Usually the elderly brigade made up of Nev, Scholesy and myself would take on Cristiano and perhaps a couple of the foreign lads. Was he the best at head-tennis? Probably he thought he was, but when you're at United you find everybody's pretty useful. It tends to be a relaxed activity in which we enjoy winding each other up, which is what's happening here. True, it can get a bit feisty towards the end when decisions might be disputed, but that's only because these kids struggle to keep up with the men of experience.

⌃ When I walked off at Goodison Park to be greeted by Sir Alex Ferguson after United had come from two down to beat Everton 4–2 near the end of the 2006/07 title race, the expression on his face told me of his belief, make that his near-certainty, that another championship was in the bag. Clearly he felt that with Chelsea only drawing that morning after leading, the balance of power had shifted.

Due to the way we were playing, I had felt confident even after going two down. Then John O'Shea pulled one back, we equalised through an own goal by Phil Neville of all people – how mortified he must have been by that – before a cute finish by Wayne Rooney and another from young Chris Eagles left us in the clear. We were gathering momentum at exactly the right time and afterwards our inner strength and determination became even more apparent in training. That lunchtime, we could smell the title. Now all we had to do was keep our nerve.

» He might look a trifle spindly on television, but in the flesh he's a giant with muscles to match and you can take it from me that when you get a bear hug from Edwin van der Sar, you really feel the squeeze. Seven days on from Goodison on another sunny Saturday morning, having suffered the midweek trauma of a debilitating Champions League defeat in Milan, we made the short journey to Eastlands for yet another crucial contest. Despite their tough defending, we were by far the better team. Michael Ball conceded a penalty which Ronaldo converted and we deserved our 1–0 lead as we approached the closing stages.

But then Wes Brown was harshly penalised and City were awarded a spot-kick. Suddenly all our good work was at risk, but we were rescued by the big Dutchman, who saved Darius Vassell's effort with his legs. Hence my feet leaving the ground in this joyful scene at the final whistle.

⌃ I'm always ready to give Gary a helping hand! This time it was after the Premiership presentation at Old Trafford in May 2007.

⌐ I'm the target for a champagne shower in the Old Trafford dressing room after the West Ham game in May 2007 because I've just been presented with my ninth Premiership medal, outstripping the previous record for title wins held by Alan Hansen and Phil Neal of Liverpool. Upending a bottle over my head is Mikael Silvestre, my good friend and yoga partner. He's a really nice bloke, very intelligent and was a fine player in his prime, a defender who was quick, strong and skilful. For some reason certain footballers go through long careers at United without quite getting the credit they deserve, and he falls into that category for me although he's moved on now.

On the right is Gaby Heinze, more of a no-nonsense performer who would stop opponents one way or another, a bit like Nemanja Vidic. In training he always gave the impression of being tired or aching, but he would usually play. In the end he lost out to the superior attacking qualities of Patrice Evra and left for Real Madrid. I got on with Gaby but he never really got to grips with the lingo, which meant he missed out on a lot of the banter.

⅃ When I fell in a heap with Chelsea keeper Petr Cech during the 2007 FA Cup final, was the ball over the goal-line? Yes, and by a long way. But referee Steve Bennett got it outrageously wrong and almost certainly his mistake cost United the trophy. It was 0–0 at the time and in these big games usually the winner is the one that scores the first goal. As it was, Didier Drogba struck near the end of extra time and Chelsea went home with the silverware.

The controversial incident happened towards the end of the first period of extra time when Wayne Rooney crossed and I was just about to finish when I was clipped from the back by Michael Essien. I stumbled into Cech but I didn't foul him and when I saw the ball cross the line I was ready to celebrate. When the referee waved play on it was not exactly my happiest Wembley moment.

CHAPTER ELEVEN

2007/08

It was a dark and stormy night . . .

>> What a cuddly little feller – and the tiger cub's pretty cute, too! In the summer of 2007 United called in at a safari park in Guangzhou, China, and I was introduced to this new friend. Pre-season is the one time footballers get the chance to see something of the countries they visit because they might be in the same place for a couple of weeks, whereas if we're abroad for, say, a Champions League game then the schedule is very tight. In China there is fanatical support for United and we were followed almost everywhere, but the safari park was cordoned off specially for us so we had time and space to relax. The only pity was that I couldn't have the kids with me to see the animals. As for my new chum, I doubt if he'd recognise me now. More likely he'd eat me.

<< When United flew off for a winter break in Saudi early in 2008 we took a stroll through a traditional Arabian village and I sampled the local mode of transport. I was offered the choice of camel or quad bike and had no hesitation in plumping for the animal. I thought that might be the easy option, but I found it quite uncomfortable. They're massive beasts which sway as they walk, and it's a weird sensation when they stand up after you've climbed aboard. Most of the lads chose camels over bikes and, amazingly enough, nobody fell off or made a fool of themselves. They were all pretty well behaved, the camels.

" Before seeing the Queen I was told exactly how to behave. "

≪ 'How's the season going? I understand you do a lot of work for UNICEF.' That was the Queen speaking, not me, when I met her to receive my OBE at Buckingham Palace in December 2007. She went on to ask me if the football was keeping me busy, though she didn't come up with any transfer gossip. I'd have been well impressed by that. Joking apart, it was a fantastic experience to meet her and certainly she gave off a very imposing aura.

Before seeing the Queen I was told exactly how to behave. I would enter the room, then when I was three yards away I would bow and walk up to her. Then I would wait to be spoken to. I was told she would let me know when she had finished, which she did, and it was a peculiar moment. She just shook my hand – she had quite a firm grip – and then she pushed me away, which was my cue to leave. That's the protocol, which obviously she knows has been communicated to me by her aides. So I stepped back, bowed again and departed. She had been extremely gracious and my audience with her seemed like ages, but probably it wasn't.

I had been to the Palace once before, to a garden party with lots of sports people and actors during the 1994 World Cup. I didn't meet the Queen then but ended up in the kitchen with Stephen Hendry, watching a game on TV. I wouldn't have got away with that this time, because Stacey was with me . . .

❝ It was one of the most difficult weeks of my Manchester United career, and certainly the most pressure I have ever felt ahead of any game. **❞**

⌃ Of course, it was entirely appropriate that the club should mark the fiftieth anniversary of the Munich air disaster, and I believe it did so with the utmost taste and respect, but I can't pretend that it didn't harm our performance when we met City at the end of that week in February 2008.

The local derby is one of the biggest matches of the season anyway, but we also had to cope with the Munich press conference and the photo sessions, which mostly involved local lads who had been with the club a long time, like Wes Brown, Paul Scholes, Gary Neville and me.

Sir Bobby Charlton came to Carrington to talk to us about the accident, and that was very moving. It made a huge impression on all of us, and brought home its significance to some of the foreign players who until then had not appreciated the full harrowing history. When we walked out for the game behind the managers, Sven-Goran Eriksson and Sir Alex Ferguson (right), the atmosphere was almost

uncanny. The eyes of the world were on us. We were under immense pressure to perform in our special kit devoid of logos, which added to the feeling of abnormality. The team just didn't turn up; we gave a poor display in the middle of some excellent ones and we lost 2–1. Normally big occasions don't bother us, but this was a one-off, a rare instance of build-up affecting the players and the whole club. In the end I think it's fair to say the emotion of the anniversary got to us.

>> After the solemnity of the Munich anniversary, this is the other end of the spectrum – a good laugh in training. Maybe the results have just come through – Liverpool have lost and City have been relegated! Actually, we were playing a game employed by our sports scientist Tony Strudwick (behind John O'Shea), the lad who warms us up ahead of matches, in this case our away encounter with Lyon. It's a bit like Simon Says, putting your hands on your shoulders, putting your hands on your knees, and so on. It tends to be funny when someone gets caught out, perhaps one of the foreign lads who's not used to it. Here Tony and Anderson have both got their hands raised and Wayne Rooney is looking quite sheepish so you can bet it's him who's messed up. Meanwhile Michael Carrick and myself are splitting our sides, while Sheasy looks as if he might burst.

JOHN O'SHEA:

I'd like to say we were laughing at Giggsy, but Wazza was the culprit here. He just couldn't get the hang of it, getting it wrong six times in a row. In the end his efforts were so funny that we stopped doing it ourselves just to watch him. Each time we expected him to do it right, but I think he got worse as the game went on.

WAYNE ROONEY:

I have to own up and admit that Giggsy and Sheasy have got me dead to rights. Our training is a serious business, but we have a bit of banter to get the lads going before a session, and I have been known to get certain exercises wrong. At least it gave them a laugh!

>> Just look at that Scholesy at Carrington, with the mischief positively oozing out of him. I can tell by the bib in his left hand that we're doing boxes, which involves two players in an eight-yard square chasing the ball, while seven or eight lads round the outside try to keep it away from them. It's all one-touch stuff and if an outsider gives the ball away or allows an insider to touch it then he replaces him. On the other hand, if an insider is nutmegged he stays in for another turn. Insiders are denoted, by the way, by clutching bibs.

Basically, this is our chance for a bit of banter before training starts in earnest. It involves loads of mickey-taking, with the outsiders trying to stitch up their mates by making their passes deliberately too hard or bouncing them awkwardly. There's nobody more devilish than Scholesy at that, though it takes a cute opponent to catch him out. Lots of arguing goes on and occasionally something which starts out as a laugh turns highly competitive. Imagine the likes of Sparky or Incey or Robbo in this situation. Or Keaney! Who's the best at it now? Well, Nev's the worst, that's easy. There are plenty who are brilliant, but if I had to choose one above the rest it would have to be Scholesy.

PAUL SCHOLES:

Ryan says I'm the best boxes player of them all? Actually, I'd say that about him as well. Everything Ryan does he does unbelievably well.

It's true that a lot of winding up goes on to get people into the box. We do get the odd angry person who refuses to go in, but not Ryan and me. We might resort to an occasional bit of mischief, but we're both honest in the box. There's a few that aren't, though!

» Keeping my eyes on the ball during my hundredth Champions League game, against Lyon in their Stade Gerland in February 2008.

" I've not been brought up to win penalties and my attitude won't change. **"**

⌄ The Gaffer has often joked with me for not going to ground for enough penalties down the years. Sometimes he'll say it's because of my balance, then again he might accuse me of being too honest. On this occasion there was no doubt: I was taken out by Everton's Steven Pienaar, shortly before Christmas 2007 with the score tied at 1–1 and only a couple of minutes to play. He's stuck his leg out, I've fallen over it and there's nothing I could do to remain on my feet.

But my instinct, always, is to stay upright so that I can score a goal or get in a cross. I've not been brought up to win penalties and my attitude won't change. Sadly, though, things are changing in the wider game, with young players arriving and some of them trying it on. They see it on the TV and they think it's OK. Not me. I'll never take a dive.

≫ 'That's how you go down for a penalty, young man!' As if he needed to be told, some might say. It had looked as if we were going to drop two points, so it was a relief to have a laugh with Cristiano Ronaldo after he's put away the spot-kick conceded by Pienaar, enabling us to beat Everton 2–1.

» Walking through the storm on my way to the bench after scoring my hundredth league goal at home to Derby in December 2007. I don't think it was a deliberate substitution so that I could get a round of applause; more likely it was the Gaffer wanting to protect my hamstrings considering the pitch was so heavy.

When the weather is as terrible as this, some people think it brings a good side down to the level of their opponents, but actually not many conditions hamper the better team. A bobbly pitch can have a bad effect, but when it's slick, United can still fizz the ball about and we've played some beautiful football in absolute downpours.

« Why the glum face? We've just conceded a late equaliser to Arsenal at the Emirates in November 2007 and I'm not a happy boy. Having got that close to winning the game, it was hugely disappointing, especially as they'd struck twice late on to nick it from us in the corresponding fixture the previous season. This time it was such a peculiar goal, too; a shot from William Gallas only just crossing the line before bouncing away, and a lot of people didn't realise it had gone in. Before the game a draw wouldn't have seemed like such a disaster, but United never expect to give away a lead.

When we've put so much into a game, but our day is absolutely ruined and we're feeling gutted, it's easy to forget our duty to acknowledge the fans. All we want to do is get off the pitch, but usually the manager or one of the more experienced lads will remind us. It's important that we don't overlook the people who follow us all over the country and who are now feeling just as fed up as the players.

⌃ It was the last day of the 2007/08 Premier League campaign, we needed to win at Wigan to be certain of retaining the title and I was on the bench. The dugout is very close to the crowd at the DW Stadium (then the JJB) and this idiot kept telling us Chelsea were 1–0 up, then 2–0, then 3–0. I had no way of knowing if he was making it up, and I must admit he had me worried. My nerves eased a bit when Cristiano put us in front from the penalty spot, but it wasn't until I scored this goal ten minutes from time that I was sure we were champions again.

I drifted to the edge of their box, Wayne slipped me the ball and I found myself through on Chris Kirkland. He's a big lad, and suddenly a piece of advice from our goalkeeping coach at the time, Richard Hartis, flashed across my mind. He'd told me that Kirkland usually stood up for one-on-ones, so to keep my shot low if possible. That's what I did, slotting it home as Maynor Figueroa (left) and Titus Bramble arrived too late to make a tackle. It was a supremely satisfying moment, especially as I had equalled Sir Bobby Charlton's United appearance record in front of our own contingent of fans in the act of securing the championship. And Chelsea? They drew 1–1 with Bolton.

" I always said that I wanted to end up with eleven championship medals because that's the number I wear on my back. **"**

» Club captain Gary Neville had been injured for most of the season and Rio Ferdinand had worn the armband when we beat Wigan to clinch the Premier League, but the Gaffer was keen for me to receive the trophy because it was my tenth title and also that day I had equalled Sir Bobby Charlton's appearance record for the club.

That was typical attention to detail by Sir Alex, and I really appreciated it. It was good of Rio to step aside, too. In Nev's absence, we had shared the captaincy throughout the campaign and it's not every day any player is handed such a prize, but the big feller just grinned and said, 'No problem.' I always said that I wanted to end up with eleven championship medals because that's the number I wear on my back, but that was when I was on seven or eight and double figures still seemed like a dream. Now? I guess I'm being greedy, but it'd be grand to reach the teens . . .

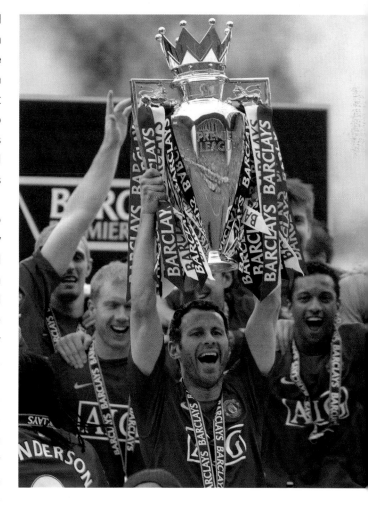

⌃ After occupying the bench for eighty-seven minutes in Moscow, I'm desperate to get on the pitch to make my contribution in the Champions League final. It's really difficult joining the action so late, especially on such a massive occasion. No matter how much you warm up on the touchline, it's hard to pick up the pace of the game, both physically and mentally. As I sat there waiting with the other subs, I watched the game very closely, wondering how I might influence it, how I might make the most telling use of all my experience. Then my number came up to replace Scholesy, the adrenaline whizzed faster than ever and I was on.

⌐ It was fantastic for Scholesy to start the final against Chelsea after missing out through suspension in 1999, and he was superb in Moscow, playing a major part, along with Wes Brown, in setting up Cristiano Ronaldo's goal. Paul broke his nose in a collision with Claude Makelele, and there was quite a bit of blood, but that was never going to get him off the pitch and he went on to demonstrate all his class and know-how before a worldwide audience. There were no words exchanged as we passed on the touchline, only a hand clasp. We both knew he'd done his bit and that it was time for me to get busy. As it turned out I couldn't make any impression on the 1–1 scoreline, so the ultimate football drama beckoned . . .

PAUL SCHOLES:

You're never ready to come off, but sometimes the manager looks to find someone to change the game. Ryan was an unbelievable sub to have on the bench, the best possible. I was just surprised he didn't start.

⩔ When you're involved in the lottery of a penalty shoot-out for the biggest prize in club football, that walk from the halfway line to the spot is long and lonely, even for someone like me who doesn't normally suffer from nerves. When John Terry stepped up, needing only to score for Chelsea to lift the trophy, I had believed it was all over for us. One of the England lads said he never missed penalties, he was really good at them, and probably if he hadn't slipped at the vital moment, his shot would have gone in instead of clipping the upright. But he did miss and now it was my turn.

I'm the first to admit that I'm not a great penalty taker, having never done the job consistently throughout my career, yet in Moscow I felt confident. Every day for a week we had taken two or three kicks each at the end of training, and my tally was thirteen hits and one miss. So when I came up against Petr Cech, who's a very big lad indeed, I knew exactly where I was going to place the ball, and as he dived one way I managed to pop it in the opposite corner. The relief was overwhelming but the tension wasn't over. Now it was down to Nicolas Anelka and Edwin van der Sar.

⌃ After what seemed an eternity suspended between ecstasy and despair, Edwin saved Anelka's penalty and in this split second the realisation has dawned that we are European champions again. What you see on the faces of Nani, myself, Patrice, Cristiano, Michael and Rio is pure, undiluted joy. We aren't saying a coherent word, just roaring our heads off and racing towards Edwin for the mother of all hugs. Only a few minutes earlier we had been facing defeat and the prospect of a dismal night. Now, though the rain continued to hammer down, there wasn't a cloud in United's sky. It didn't

matter that we'd won in a shoot-out; all that mattered was that the big-eared monster of a trophy would be going back to Manchester.

For me it was different to how I'd felt nine years earlier when we won in Barcelona. I was crying in the Nou Camp, overwhelmed by emotion, and so much of the experience passed me by. But in Moscow I was more mature, able to take everything in, and I relished every last drop of the euphoria. What was similar about the two occasions was that both had felt like a ride on a crazy roller-coaster, which made the ultimate fulfilment seem that much sweeter.

⌃ To be in the midst of this ticker-tape blizzard, with all the noise and the cascading tinsel, and in the company of these lads who had been striving towards this goal for so long, was like walking into a fantasy. The rain was bucketing down but that didn't bother us in the slightest; you can only get so wet and then the water simply runs off you. We just wanted to savour the moment and to share it with the fans. I urged the younger players to imprint this scene on their memories, which should increase their motivation to repeat the triumph in the near future. I had to wait nine years between European Cups, and that's too long.

⌃ Where on earth did Patrice get that hat? Maybe it was thrown into the air and landed on the pitch when Edwin made his save, or perhaps he nicked it off someone's head – I don't suppose he had a clue either way.

Whenever United win something big, I always try to have pictures taken with the people I've worked with closely, and certainly that applies to Pat. He is so quick and clever, and playing immediately behind me at left back he adds that penetration which I don't supply so often any more because I'm not as quick as I used to be. We complement each other ideally, and as we clasped the spoils of victory I was telling him what a great season he'd had and how brilliant he'd been for me. I'm not being biased when I describe him as one of the best left backs in the world. Having faced Pat so often in training, I can honestly say that he's harder to play against than Ashley Cole.

He's a smashing bloke, too, very lively around the club. He's always doing impressions of the other lads, and he's extremely popular.

⌄ If it wasn't for the beaming grins, I'd say the dressing room in Moscow resembled a battlefield after the match. Certainly it was mucky enough. You can always tell the experienced players in a situation like this. As soon as they get in, they put a towel over their blazers because they know the champagne corks will be popping and the bubbly will be flying everywhere. The young ones have to learn the hard way.

⌃ It was a piece of the purest serendipity. On the afternoon we won the league I equalled Sir Bobby Charlton's Manchester United record of 758 appearances for the club, and on the night we lifted the European Cup I beat it. This didn't go unnoticed by my team-mates, who rounded off a perfect ten days for me by asking Sir Bobby to present me with a watch inscribed with the new mark, 759, at our hotel in Moscow as the celebrations showed no sign of abating in the early hours of the morning.

After the game in Barcelona nine years earlier, the last time we became European champions, I was legless and can't recall too much about the proceedings. This time, being that much more grown-up, I just had a couple of beers and soaked up the whole experience. My moment came after we'd been back at the hotel for an hour or so, when the club chief executive David Gill picked up the mike and asked all the players and staff, except Ryan, to go on the stage. I was the only person in the room without a clue about what was going on, but soon it became clear as David, Sir Alex and then Sir Bobby said some nice things about me and presented me with the beautiful watch. Meanwhile all the lads were having a laugh, singing catchy little ditties like 'Giggs will tear you apart again' and 'Ryan Giggs, Ryan Giggs, running down the wing' at the top of their voices. Unbelievable.

In fact, it wouldn't have worked out so perfectly but for the vigilance of the club statistician, Cliff Butler. A few months earlier he had spotted that one of the appearances previously credited to Sir Bobby had actually been made by the late Warren Bradley, so he adjusted the figures and when Moscow ticked around everything fell into place. Thanks for that, mate, I owe you a beer.

SIR BOBBY CHARLTON:

When the players asked me to present Ryan with the watch, it was a huge pleasure to oblige. He's very popular with everyone at the club, both as a smashing lad and a magnificent footballer. I was delighted that he had passed my milestone, especially as it happened on such a perfect night, and nobody could have deserved it more. The atmosphere at the Moscow celebration do was brilliant and nobody got too drunk – or I suppose they might have done after I'd gone to bed!

>> Totally knackered but still walking – make that staggering – on air, the United party arrive back in Manchester with the two most important trophies in the club game firmly in our custody. Despite the fact that we'd had precious little sleep, the Gaffer looks bright-eyed and bushy-tailed, while Rio and I are wondering how we're going to make it down the steps of the plane.

CHAPTER TWELVE

2008/09

The one that got away

"I'm still not completely convinced about the headgear . . . "

« When I was told that the University of Salford had selected me to receive an honorary degree in 2007, I wondered how I might look in a mortarboard and gown, and now I know! It meant the world to me to be honoured like this in a city which is, and will always remain, so close to my heart. I'm still not completely convinced about the headgear, though.

∧ I don't know if the train was late, but I'm looking a little impatient and making a call from the bench at Stockport station. We travel to London by rail, with most of the lads climbing aboard at Stockport, a few more embarking at Wilmslow. If the game is on a Saturday, our Friday ritual is to train at Carrington, then go home for an hour or so before meeting again at the station. There are always lots of photographers there. When we're in public, we're never free of them.

≪ A quick cuddle with Wayne Rooney at the final whistle after he'd scored the only goal of the local derby at Eastlands in November 2008. He was already maturing by then, willing to stand up and take responsibility in the really big games, but it's since the departure of Cristiano Ronaldo that he has truly blossomed. He always had remarkable ability, but now he seems in command of it all, getting the best out of himself. He has become a regular match-winner. In 2009/10 he was scoring goals for fun with his head, more of which seems to be visible these days . . .

≫ This was not my finest hour. The scene was another of those sunny Saturday lunchtimes at Anfield, this time in September 2008, and the score was 1–1 with about fifteen minutes left to play. Liverpool were on the attack and I thought I was shepherding the ball to safety, but Javier Mascherano got his toe in and crossed to Ryan Babel, who scored the winner.

I wasn't looking forward to going back to the dressing room at the end and facing the manager, but actually he was quite restrained. He told me that a player of my experience should have put the ball out for a corner – or words to that effect! To be fair, when a player makes a bad error, missing a chance or costing a goal, Sir Alex understands that everyone makes mistakes occasionally, and he knows me well enough to be aware that I'll be feeling hugely disappointed myself. What really gets his goat is if a player doesn't do what he's been told, perhaps repeatedly. That's when things get heated and the sparks can fly. Luckily, this time it was early in the season and there was plenty of time to come back. It spoiled my weekend, though.

A Club World Cup Japan 2008 presented by

⌃ There were plenty of critics who dissed the Club World Championship, but nobody should be in any doubt that Manchester United were deadly serious about it. After all, you have to win the Champions League just to qualify, so it's hardly small beer. We were all desperate to beat the Ecuadorian club, Quito, in the Yokohama final just before Christmas 2008, and when we won, thanks to a goal from Wayne Rooney, we were ecstatic. Just look at the manager on the far right. He's like a kid, singing in the tinsel.

⌝ There's not a handbag in sight, but fingers are being pointed meaningfully as Phil Neville and I indulge in a brisk exchange of views during our 1–1 draw with Everton at Goodison Park in October 2008. My old United mate had just taken out Cristiano – perhaps I had better say tackled! – when the Portuguese was on the floor. It's not my way to get angry, but as skipper I'm standing up for my team-mate, while Phil contends that he won the ball. Happily we could have that clash without any lingering ill will because we both understand that disagreements on the pitch are part of the game.

I was sorry when Phil left Old Trafford, and I felt the same about Nicky Butt. They are both tremendous players and close friends, but in both cases I could understand that they made wise football decisions. It's not nice seeing your mates disappointed every other week because they're not in the team. Phil has done brilliantly at Everton, where he is now the captain. He's been totally accepted there, which can't have been easy after all his years at United. He's a true pro, too, living his life the right way, going to bed at 9.30 every night. Phil always made friends with the foreign players, taking the mick and making them feel at home. He's a terrific lad, though totally different to brother Gary. He's less confrontational, less intense and definitely less talkative.

PHIL NEVILLE:

Giggsy is always the first to get round the referee when there's a bit of controversy, and he's got such a scary glare that you think he might be about to rip your head off. I'd done a tackle on Cristiano and it was ironic that the first two men on the scene trying to make sure I was punished were two of my oldest friends in the game, Giggsy and Scholesy.

As we were growing up at United, Giggsy was always the elder statesman of our group. He knows I'm three years younger and that he can get at me with those eyes. He's well aware of the effect it can have on me, so he plays on it even more. What passed between us here? I said I'd got the ball, he said I hadn't, so I just shut up! We had a laugh about it straight afterwards, but when the game is on there are no friendships. It was a case of both of us wanting our team to win – and Giggsy's the biggest winner of all time.

⌃ There weren't enough funny hats to go round, but that didn't materially hinder the celebrations after we had beaten Spurs on penalties to win the 2009 League Cup at Wembley. Cristiano loves a party, and he threw himself into it with all his usual energy. The game was a fairly disappointing 0–0 draw, which was peculiar because usually our meetings with Tottenham are full of excitement and good football. Still, it was great to bag our second trophy of the season, following the Club World Championship, on the first day of March and we felt we were gathering momentum at just the right time.

» Here's a piece of free advice. Always wrap up warm when your work takes you to Newcastle, particularly if your job involves sitting down in the open air. When United called at St James' Park in March 2009, the wind whistling round that magnificent stadium came straight off the North Sea, there was a dusting of snow on the pitch and ice in my boots. I took the precaution of wearing several layers under my tracksuit top, but this was an occasion on which I envied Sir Bobby Charlton the fur hat he invariably sports on winter nights.

" Always wrap up warm when your work takes you to Newcastle . . . **"**

⌃ There have been few more satisfying goals in my career than this one, scored at Upton Park in February 2009, not least because it was the only strike of a tense encounter and it took us back to the top of the Premiership table. Oddly enough, this was one of those few occasions these days when I started on the right, yet the goal materialised after I popped up on the left for virtually the only time in the game.

We had just taken a corner, the ball reached Scholesy in the middle and he pinged it out to me. It was one of those passes where he barely had to look; he just sensed me there. At first I was looking to get in a cross, but the defender dived in so I kept dummying until I saw a gap appear at the far post. I hit it with my right foot, low and hard through a crowd of players, and it went exactly where it was intended, which isn't always the case with my 'swinger'. The goal came after an hour in which I didn't think I'd played particularly well, but this turned my afternoon around.

It can be hostile at West Ham, something I've noticed since my early days. There was a history with Incey and bad feeling about Becks, after he was sent off in the 1998 World Cup. The crowd always used to be right on top of you, although there's a bit more space now, but they are real football supporters who know their stuff and the atmosphere is always terrific.

» A linesman is caught cold, and Wayne Rooney and I are definitely not amused. It happened against Chelsea at Old Trafford in January 2009, just before the interval with the game goalless. Wayne took a corner by just touching the ball out of the quadrant, then walked away. Nobody noticed but as I passed him he whispered that the ball was in play, so I ran in with it, crossed and Cristiano nodded it into the net. But then the linesman, Darren Cann, flagged and a goal we thought was perfectly legitimate was ruled out. Quite simply, I believe the official got it horribly wrong. Didn't he wonder why I was running in with the ball? Did he think I'd lost my marbles or what?

The only mistake we made was Wayne not telling the linesman that he had taken the corner. We had done it a few times in training, we believed it was legal and now it was monumentally frustrating to pull it off in such an important game only to be denied. Happily, moral justice was done because we scored almost straight afterwards from another set-piece, Nemanja Vidic heading in from my delivery and we went on to win 3–0. Since then I've joked with Darren Cann about not allowing short corners at the World Cup, where he proved he's a top official by his selection for the final.

WAYNE ROONEY:

I admit I was furious because we didn't believe we had broken any rules and the goal should have been allowed to stand. But Giggsy was diplomatic as always, trying to persuade the linesman to think back, and we didn't go over the top with our protest. On reflection, I should have mentioned to the official that I had taken the kick, but I overlooked that in the heat of the game.

⌃ This was a big moment on the way to our third successive title in May 2009. Middlesbrough weren't doing too well in the table but they always gave us a tough game at the Riverside and for the first twenty-five minutes this proved to be no exception. But then Kiko Macheda got the ball on the edge of their box, shielded it and rolled it for me to hit first time through the legs of David Wheater into the corner of the net.

≫ I'm not waving to our own fans after the goal, but to the Boro contingent who had been taking the rise out of me – good-naturedly, it has to be said – only a few moments earlier. This game was a week after I'd received the PFA Player of the Year award, and as I took a corner they were chanting, 'Player of the year, you're having a laugh.' The whole stand joined in and I couldn't help smiling because it was genuinely funny. But when I scored immediately afterwards, I did think a little wave was in order.

Also appreciating the joke is Kiko, a really confident lad of whom the manager has high expectations. He made his entrance that season with a goal to die for, the late winner at home to Aston Villa, and that was typical of a player who doesn't always take the eye in general play but who comes alive in the box. Kiko's a bit like Ruud van Nistelrooy in that he scores goals of every description, and although he had a frustrating time with injury in 2009/10, if he works hard he must have a chance of making the grade with United.

>> Three old geezers striking a familiar pose in the Old Trafford dressing room, this time after clinching the Premiership in 2009 thanks to an extremely tense goalless draw with Arsenal. Nev is my best mate at United. He's always got an opinion and he's ready to speak his mind; he always wants the best for his team-mates and he's United to the core. Of course, because he personifies United and no other club matters to him, he's the man opposition supporters love to hate. But if they tell the truth, they would have to say they'd have liked him as their regular right back for the last fifteen years.

Then there's the side of Gary which is never publicised. He's a clever lad, very sharp, and he does a lot to help youngsters with contracts, pensions, investments, that sort of thing. He gets a lot of stick because he takes no rubbish. True, he does get on your nerves because he talks too much, and I do wish he'd shut up just occasionally. But I guess that's wishful thinking and we'll simply have to go on loving him the way he is.

PAUL SCHOLES:

It's difficult to believe we're still there winning things after all these years. At one point I'd have been happy just to win one trophy. Still, they've kept on coming, and even now I hope there's more to win. Ryan's one of the oldest at the club now, but the others don't take the mick out of him for that. Too much respect? There's that, but also he doesn't act like an old player – and they can't catch him.

GARY NEVILLE:

There's a special bond between the lads who came through the ranks together. Ryan is a unique individual whose achievements will never be repeated. He combines professionalism with style, skill, speed, longevity – he's the complete package. Throughout his career he's always shown great humility, and he's liked by pretty well everyone in the country, stretching way beyond our own club. In fact, you might say he is completely the opposite of myself in that sense! We've had Sir Matt, Sir Alex and Sir Bobby, and one day I should imagine we'll be talking about Sir Ryan.

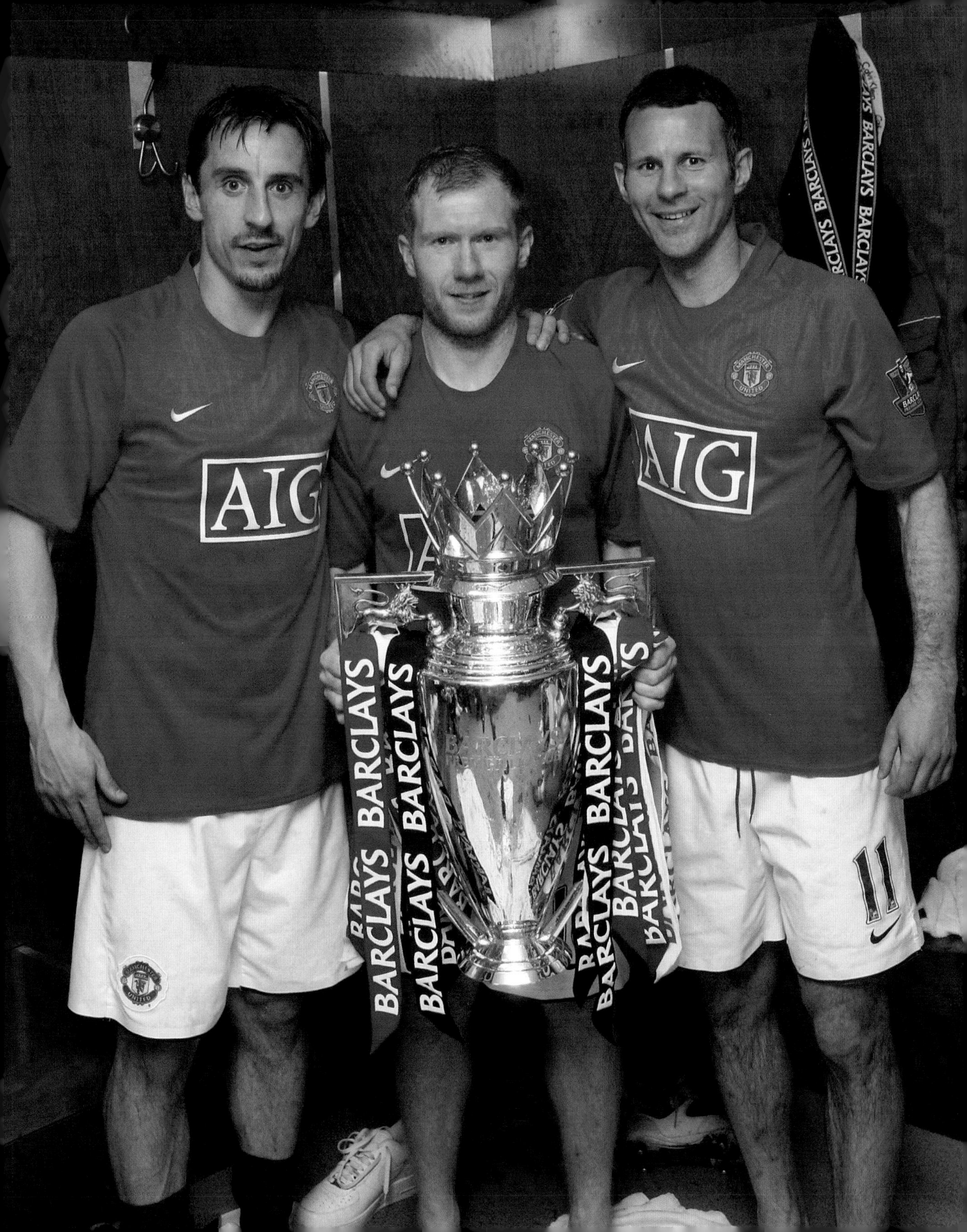
AIG
AIG
AIG
BARCLAYS

⌃ The atmosphere at Parkhead was on fire. Five minutes from time in our Champions League clash with Celtic in November 2008 we were a goal behind, despite absolutely battering them for most of the second half. It was beginning to look as if we'd never break through when I saw Cristiano lining up for one of his specials and I darted forward just in case there was a rebound. The shot moved all over the place, Celtic keeper Artur Boruc could only parry it and I was on the spot to nod in the rebound. It was one of those where I knew I'd clatter into the post if someone pushed me, so I just got my head to it and took cover. It was fantastic to pull off a piece of opportunism like that right in front of the United fans, who went mad. The stadium isn't as big as Old Trafford but it's got to be the noisiest I've played in, along with Ibrox and the Turkish grounds of Besiktas and Fenerbahce. What with the Gaffer being Scottish and a former Rangers man, it was some occasion.

≫ Sir Alex Ferguson is a man in his element at Carrington. Sometimes I think he gets as much knowledge, and as much fun, out of watching us train as he does from a game. After all, everything is done at match pace, it can be very fierce, and often the quality on display is unbelievable. There is never any holding back; everybody is doing their utmost to stake their claim for a place on the team, and I think the manager thrives on all that. The day before a game the training tends to be a bit lighter to lessen the risk of injuries, and the poles come out, as seen here, for a few relay races.

For all that we're very busy and professional, there is always time for a laugh, and the Gaffer loves to join in. You get the odd player who will take the mick out of him. I might have a (very) gentle go occasionally, but Wayne gets away with a little more, as Yorkie always used to. It's a question of Sir Alex assessing all the different characters and treating them accordingly. For instance, he would approach Eric Cantona one way and Lee Sharpe another. It's called man management and it's a big part of his genius.

I'm in my Carrington training gear, bearing my personal number which I was given when I joined as an apprentice and have kept throughout my career. It's on all my kit so I can make sure I get the right stuff when it comes back from the laundry. It's a far cry from the ancient days when, apparently, the training kit was not washed so frequently and often remained in a heap in the dressing room, which meant it was a case of first come, first served when the players arrived in the morning.

" The banter was flying as it always has down the years. **"**

>> David Beckham will be a massive Manchester United fan as long as he lives, and it was no surprise when he dropped into the Emirates dressing room after we'd beaten Arsenal in the semi-final of the Champions League in the spring of 2009. He's very close to Gary Neville, they speak all the time, and although I'm not in regular contact with him we're still mates and it was a pleasure to see him again, especially after such a brilliant win. Becks loves United so much – as does his dad, who never misses a game, home or away – and he was delighted to catch us on a night when we were really on song. Of course, the banter was flying as it always has down the years. I couldn't possibly see Becks and not take the mick out of what he was wearing.

GARY NEVILLE:

The greatest thing about playing for United over the last fifteen years has been the friendships formed, especially between the six of us who stayed at the club for such a long time. It was tremendous to catch up with David at the Emirates, and the mick-taking resumed as though we'd never been apart. We might have been discussing David's clothes but, more likely, how Ryan's losing his chest hair!

DAVID BECKHAM:

This was the first time I had seen United play since leaving the club. It was an honour to be there and see the friends I had grown up with perform the way they did. After the game I went to the dressing room to say hello. Nothing had changed, the banter was still the same. On the clothes front, Giggsy cannot even comment after some of the jackets he used to wear with Incey – and he could do with losing some of his chest hair, to be honest!

⌃ Looking solemn before kick-off in the 2009 Champions League final – and we might have appeared even more serious if we had known what was coming that night in Rome. We knew Barcelona were a great team but certainly we didn't expect the game to go the way it did. The year before, if anything, we were slight underdogs against Chelsea, but this time we were just about favourites. After all, we had beaten them in the 2008 semi-final, and now for the first ten minutes we looked good once again. But it was one of those games where one team scores and the opposition never quite recovers from it. Still, at half-time we remained confident and focused; the talk was all about playing better and there was genuine belief that we could. We achieved some slight improvement but we didn't get anywhere near what we had produced throughout the season, which was a crushing disappointment.

The sombre line-up is, back row left to right: Edwin van der Sar, Nemanja Vidic, Rio Ferdinand, John O'Shea, Anderson, Cristiano Ronaldo. Front row: me, Michael Carrick, Wayne Rooney, Patrice Evra, Ji-Sung Park.

At the final whistle, everyone was in shock, not only at the result but also at the performance. We just didn't see it coming and it was hard to take. Unfortunately it was the last match of the season, which left us no chance to recover. We'd won the Premiership again but this was the game that would remain in our heads. A win doesn't last the summer, but when you get beaten it lasts a lot longer.

As we stand disconsolately on the pitch, nobody looking more fed up than the Gaffer, we're mulling over how tough it had been to get to the final, recalling particularly the tremendous efforts against Inter Milan and Arsenal. It was a campaign which should have ended on the highest note, but instead here we were plumbing the depths of despair. I hadn't felt that bad since we lost the league title to Leeds in 1992 at the end of my first full season. I was woefully disappointed, both with my own personal display and the way the team had played. The only positive aspect was that I believed we could use the experience as motivation to prevent it happening again, and so move forward.

⌃ I'd never met Jeff Stelling before the night I received the PFA Player of the Year award in 2009, but I had always admired his work on Sky TV's *Soccer Saturday*, on which he does such an incredible job. Though he's got scores and stories and chat coming at him from all directions, he's funny and he's bubbly and he very rarely makes a mistake.

I couldn't hope to compete with such a professional when I stepped up to the mike, but I hope I conveyed how delighted I was to be honoured by my fellow footballers no fewer than seventeen years on from when I was selected as Young Player of the Year in 1992. To be honest, you don't really expect to win things like this in your mid-thirties when there are so many other outstanding candidates. In fact, there were some critics who reckoned I didn't deserve it because I didn't play enough games in the season, but I think that was harsh. I made twenty-eight Premiership appearances out of a maximum thirty-eight, which wasn't too bad. Overall I felt that I'd played pretty well, too, but even though nice things had been written about me in some of the newspapers, the award still came as a shock.

SIR ALEX FERGUSON:

This is the ultimate accolade for a player and no one deserved it more than Ryan. Journalists of today are adept at whipping players up to a high status, then knocking them down a wee bit, but when your own peers choose you for an award, then it's really special and means a lot more.

« My wife Stacey always comes with me to the United Player of the Year awards dinner at Old Trafford, but basically she's not too bothered about football. When I ring her after a game she might ask how we've done, but she's not going to get carried away by the state of the title race or become outraged over some controversial incident. If she happened to watch a game with a few friends, she might make a comment, but most likely it would be something girlie like: 'Why does everyone go on about Cristiano? He's not as good as you.' As for me being away from home so often because of football, it's not a problem for her. It's my job, that's the way things are, and she just gets on with it.

CHAPTER THIRTEEN

2009/10

Still hungry after all these years

⌃ I'm overjoyed at the end of the most astonishing Manchester derby of my lifetime, the one in September 2009 when we beat City 4–3 thanks to a beautiful finish by Michael Owen in the ninety-sixth minute. There had been a huge build-up, with City spending all that money and being labelled as potential champions, Sparky coming back to Old Trafford as their boss, their signing of Carlos Tevez, and then Sir Alex capping it all off by calling them the noisy neighbours. We'd always been top dogs, but now they had genuinely good players who commanded respect.

That's how the scene was set and the action unfolded so dramatically, ending up perfectly for us. I set up Michael's goal, but it was his exquisite movement which made all the difference. When the ball came to me I controlled it and looked up, sensing that they were knackered, out on their feet. Then I made a decent little pass into the box for Michael. They should have had their tails up because they had just bounced back to 3–3 after looking as though they were beaten. But you need experience of seeing out a game from there and perhaps one or two of them didn't have it. We took advantage big time.

>> It was strange to see Carlos Tevez on the other side when City arrived at Old Trafford for the first of four local derbies during 2009/10. After all, he had just spent two hugely successful seasons with us and the fans loved him. They always identify with footballers who work as hard as Carlos. He never seemed to stop scurrying around all over the place and he scored plenty of important goals into the bargain.

Of course, coming across former team-mates in the opposition is a common occurrence and players tend to shrug it off, just getting on with their jobs, but this time there was a bit more to it because of all the controversy surrounding his move across Manchester. Certainly, our manager didn't take too kindly to the 'Welcome to Manchester' poster in the city centre although I doubt if Carlos had any input into that. It was done to wind us up, but it didn't upset me. I just thought it was pretty stupid.

For all that, I was delighted that he made it clear by his friendly demeanour at the end of the game that he didn't hold any grudge against the United players. Although he struggled to master English, he understood most of what was said to him and I got on with him okay. He remains a terrific player whose work-rate is phenomenal – just look at the sweat on his shirt – and it's not surprising that he has benefited from having an extended run in the team. He wasn't getting that at United following the arrival of Dimitar Berbatov, and he didn't enjoy warming the bench.

⌃ This goal took a lot of the heat out of our game at Stoke in September 2009, coming when we were already a goal up with about a quarter of an hour left on the clock. It wasn't a routine we had perfected in training but there was a slight element of planning, because just before I took this free- kick from the right wing, John O'Shea had told me he was going to make a run towards the front post. Often from this position I aim to curl the ball towards the far post, so that it might creep in if nobody gets a touch.

That makes it horribly difficult for the keeper, with so many bodies moving about in front of him. Probably this time the ball wasn't going in, although I had put a heavy curl on it, but it didn't matter because Sheasy timed his run beautifully and directed a glancing header into the top of their net. He doesn't score many but there have been some important ones, including a winner at Anfield and one at home to Arsenal in the semi-final of the 2009 Champions League. Then there was that delightful chip at Highbury a few seasons back, one he never lets us forget.

JOHN O'SHEA:

Normally before free kicks from a wide position I'll have a word with Giggsy about making a run. Sometimes he listens to me and sometimes he doesn't. This time he did and it paid off.

When you don't score often it's a great occasion when you do, and Sheasy is enjoying himself here, lifting me off the ground as the other lads close in for a celebration. It's never easy to win at Stoke, who play in front of the noisiest crowd in the Premier League. From the moment you walk on to the pitch the din is relentless, and it gets louder every time you make the tiniest mistake.

❯ Another year, another contract extension, another season and a half at Old Trafford, at least . . .

This time I sat down with Manchester United chief executive David Gill to put pen to paper shortly before Christmas 2009, which was ideal because it meant I could concentrate purely on football for the immediate future. I'm always pleased to sign, and over the last few years it's become an increasingly relaxed piece of business. I've had to get my head around the fact that these days the Gaffer won't use me in every match, that sometimes I'm going to be rested, maybe even get the odd day off training. I think the benefits of that approach have been evident over the past few seasons and, at my vast age, it suits me fine.

⌐ To meet Del Deanus is an incredibly humbling, yet also uplifting experience. Del was a team-mate of Nicky Barmby and myself when we played for England Schoolboys back in the late 1980s, and it came as a numbing shock to learn that he has been struck down with motor neurone disease, a devastating terminal condition which meant that he couldn't walk or even move his arms at the time of writing. Yet when Nicky and I met up with him at Carrington to help publicise his new book *Memories Never Die*, which he wrote to increase awareness of the cruel illness and to raise money to fight it, he was joking and full of banter, the same old Del we had played alongside more than twenty years ago.

I met him first at the England trials, where the Cockneys stood out from the northerners because they were more flashy, louder, at the centre of everything, and Del was typical of that. He was instantly likeable and turned out to be a natural at organising other players from his position of centre half. He went on to spend four years with Spurs, and although he didn't come through at White Hart Lane he stayed in football and became the joint manager of Enfield Town, who play in the Ryman Division One North.

Remarkably given his condition, he didn't miss a match, and until 2010 played a key role at the club, where his indomitable spirit was an inspiration to everyone. Like me, Del is a dad – his daughter Megan was born on Christmas Eve 2009 – and it's unbelievably poignant to find an old team-mate in such a plight. The way he has dealt with his misfortune is a lesson to us all, and I am proud to know him.

» I expect all the winners have said this but, hand on heart, I didn't think I had a chance in a million of becoming the BBC Sports Personality of the Year. Naturally, I felt honoured to be nominated along with nine others, but I was convinced Jenson Button was a shoo-in for the award, so much so that I thought seriously about not attending the ceremony. It was on a Sunday night in Sheffield just before Christmas 2009; we were playing a couple of days later and nowadays I do need my rest, so I said to my business manager Harry Swales, 'Look, I've got no chance of winning and I could do with putting my feet up.' But Harry wouldn't hear of it. He said even if I didn't win I needed to be there and, of course, he was right as usual.

As the day approached I kept bumping into people who said they'd voted for me, but still I believed Jenson was a racing certainty and it was only on the night, when he was announced as runner-up, that the thought flashed across my mind that I might have won. Still, I was dumbfounded when my name was read out, and by then it was far too late to work on my speech!

« Considering that the last person to be awarded the Freedom of Salford was Nelson Mandela, and previous recipients include L. S. Lowry and David Lloyd George, I felt overwhelmingly privileged when my name was added to the list in January 2010. I'm a proud Welshman, but I've lived in Salford for thirty years and the place has become a huge part of me. Of course, when the news came out all my friends were making the usual jokes about being able to drive my sheep through the streets of the city, but I was most fascinated by the notion that if I was ever sentenced to be hanged, it could be by a silk scarf instead of a rope. Well, that's a comfort . . .

» If my business manager Harry Swales – seen here at Old Trafford having a laugh with Sir Bobby Charlton and me – looks like a larger-than-life character, that's because he is. I count myself so lucky to have been put in touch with him near the beginning of my career by Bryan Robson, one of the most generous and selfless people in the game.

The first time I met Harry was in the manager's office at our old training ground, the Cliff in Broughton. He was in his late sixties at the time, just recovering from a quadruple heart bypass, but he was full of life, even pulling up his trouser legs to show me his operation scars.

In his time he has worked with the England team and Kevin Keegan as well as Robbo, and it speaks volumes for him that he has the total respect of Sir Alex Ferguson. Harry is decidedly old-school in his outlook – we have never signed a contract, being content just to shake hands and trust each other, which is enough for both of us.

To be still working hard in his eighties is quite an achievement and I'm happy to say that his judgement remains as clear and sound and based on solid principles as ever. These days, quite simply, I look on Harry as part of my family, and I feel part of his.

SIR BOBBY CHARLTON:

I've known Harry for a long, long time, going back to an era when nobody thought about football agents. He might be even older than Ryan! They are two lovely characters who are just right for each other, and Ryan couldn't have had a better man to look after him.

HARRY SWALES:

I can't begin to put into words what an immense privilege and pleasure it has been to be closely associated with these two great gentlemen of sport. Throughout his career Ryan has been a joy to deal with, while Bobby and I have often worked together on charity projects. I'm so proud to know them both so well.

❝I look on Harry as part of my family, and I feel part of his.❞

» There were only three games left and we trailed Chelsea so we had to beat Spurs at Old Trafford as we chased what would have been a record nineteenth league championship in the spring of 2010. In all my time at United I had never taken a penalty in a league game, but with Wayne Rooney injured, both Nani and myself had been practising in training. We said we'd see who felt up for it on the day, and Nani felt good, but as captain and elder statesman I decided to pull rank.

I could never have imagined that there would be two spot-kicks, but after putting the first one to Heurelho Gomes's right, I was confident of sticking the other one to his left, and that's how it worked out. I admit there were a few nerves, but you have to trust the work you have put in on the training ground. We have always had top penalty-takers during my time at the club, people like Steve Bruce, Eric Cantona, Cristiano Ronaldo and now Wayne, and I've always been happy to leave the job to them, but on this occasion I felt it was up to me to accept the responsibility.

Scholesy looks relieved that I managed to knock in the first one (above) and the camera has caught the look of intense concentration on my face as I tuck away the second (right). Previously the only other penalties I'd taken for United had been in shoot-outs, and I even managed to miss one of them, at Southampton in the FA Cup.

In the end, the pair against Spurs didn't count for much as the title slipped away to Stamford Bridge. That was truly agonising, but we have a deep and talented squad of players at Old Trafford and, although there might be new and difficult tests in store, I'm certain we'll be back in serious contention for the big prizes over the seasons to come. As I write this ahead of the 2010/11 campaign my thirty-seventh birthday is looming, but I feel I still have plenty to offer the cause. OK, I'm in my third decade as a Manchester United footballer, but I feel fit and, crucially, I'm every bit as enthusiastic and hungry for success as I was on my first day at the club. A new challenge? Bring it on!

CHAPTER FOURTEEN

1991/92 2006/07

This land is dear to me

« A study in anticipation on the bench in Nuremberg in October 1991, about to become the youngest player in Welsh international history at seventeen years and eleven months. There were only about five minutes left to play in a crucial European Championship qualifier against the German side and we were getting battered 4–1 when I was called on as a substitute for Eric Young. Obviously it was a big deal for a teenager, but I didn't feel overawed. Having United team-mates Mark Hughes and Clayton Blackmore in the Welsh set-up helped me to settle, and I felt pretty comfortable with the whole experience. I didn't like the result, though.

» Sprinting like a madman after scoring my first international goal, with Gary Speed in hot pursuit ready for a celebration. It put us in front in a World Cup qualifier against the eventual group winners, Belgium, in Cardiff in March 1993 and it was particularly satisfying because it came from a direct free kick for which I had been practising hard in the run-up to the game. My goal came after eighteen minutes, Rushie added a second just before half-time and we ran out worthy 2–0 winners against very strong opponents.

It was hugely frustrating that we didn't qualify for the finals in the United States, missing out by a single point. Our fate was almost certainly decided when poor Paul Bodin hit the bar with a penalty against Romania at Cardiff in a game we went on to lose 2–1. I'm not blaming Paul, it could have happened to anybody, but we were all gutted by the experience. Who knows what might have happened, and what the impact on Welsh football might have been, if we'd gone through?

» I enjoyed working under Terry Yorath (right) and Peter Shreeves, my first management team at full international level. They made an excellent partnership, both of them passionate about their football but with contrasting personalities, Terry being fairly quiet while Peter was a

bubbly individual who did the majority of the talking. He was both a terrific coach who was full of ideas and an ideal link between the players and the boss. The pair of them made me feel at home right from the start in a team of mainly older, more experienced players, and one that was really flying. It was a pleasure to run on to the pitch alongside the likes of Ian Rush, Mark Hughes, Neville Southall, Kevin Ratcliffe and company, and I learned an enormous amount from them.

⌃ I've just managed to get my shot away under a challenge from two Italian defenders in a European Championship qualifier at Anfield in September 1998, but I'm afraid I didn't score. I did hit the crossbar with a free kick when the game was still goalless, but that wasn't much help and we lost 2–0. In the end it was crushing disappointment. We didn't even come close to making the finals, and it was the same sad and sorry story throughout most of my time with Wales. I felt my international experience started well under Terry Yorath, but somehow the team lost its way during the reigns of Mike Smith and Bobby Gould before getting back on track with Mark Hughes.

⌄ This was one of the happiest moments of my decade and a half in international football. The final whistle had blown in Minsk, where we had just beaten Belarus 2–1 in a Euro 2000 qualifier. It was Mark Hughes's first game in sole charge of the team, I had scored the winner four minutes from the end and suddenly Wales's future looked a whole lot brighter.

I knew Sparky so well and respected him so much from our time together at United, but it wasn't only me who was delighted that he was the new boss in succession to Bobby Gould, even though it was his first job in management. He brought in Mark Bowen and Eddie Niedzwiecki as coaches, and suddenly we had a tremendously professional set-up that we could all believe in. Sparky didn't say a lot, but when he spoke people listened, and everyone wanted to play for him.

⌃ I suppose it was one of the more bizarre statistics of a Wales career which began back in 1991, but this encounter with Finland at the Millennium Stadium in March 2000 – the new stadium's inaugural international match – was the first time I played in a friendly for my country. I took quite a bit of flak for missing games down the years, but that didn't bother me unduly. The fact was that as a youngster I had plenty on my plate, and then all too soon I started suffering from hamstring injuries. I faced a constant dilemma: did I play a friendly on the Wednesday, knowing that I was increasing the risk of tweaking my hamstrings, or did I take the inevitable stick for opting out?

Unfortunately we lost 2–1 to Finland, but this was something of a high spot for me, shooting past Liverpool's Sami Hyypia to reduce the arrears.

⌐ I was always proud to play for my country, but there were times, many times, when it was not exactly a barrel of laughs. Nearly everything about the international experience was marvellous – going home to see my family in Wales, spending time with some great lads, seeing a bit of the world on away trips. But all too often the only disappointing aspect was the game itself. I was not used to losing so often, which I found to be overwhelmingly frustrating, and sometimes it was difficult to understand the way we set out to play. Perhaps, also, I simply tried too hard on occasions.

⌐ I've always believed that everything had to be perfect for Wales to reach an international tournament, and on 16 October 2002 at the Millennium Stadium, that's exactly how it was. We played our hearts out, straining every sinew and performing brilliantly to beat Italy 2–1 in a European Championship qualifier, thus setting a benchmark which, alas, we could never meet on a consistent basis. Such was the injury situation that that team never even played together again, and we just didn't have the depth in our squad to make up for high-quality absentees.

But I shall always treasure the memory of how it was at the Millennium that night, overturning one of the best teams in the world. The atmosphere was fabulous, the noise was unbelievable and it was matched by the football on the pitch. The whole place was consumed by patriotism, and so was I. Sadly more disappointment was in store. We came agonisingly close to qualifying for the Euro 2004 finals, only to lose to Russia after a play-off.

⌃ It was a weird experience for me when Wales met England in a World Cup qualifier at Old Trafford in October 2004. I was being marked by Gary Neville, while Butty and Becks were both up against me, too. There I was in my home stadium, playing in a massive game, with my three best mates in football trying to do me down. Surreal or what? Of course, there was nothing else for it but to knuckle down and do the most professional job I could.

Unfortunately, England were by far the stronger side and I barely touched the ball because we could hardly ever get it off them. Still, I did manage to nutmeg both Butty and Nev, which was just about all I could take out of a pretty dismal 2–0 defeat. Certainly Becks is looking happier than me here, giving me a bit of banter while I moan at the linesman.

≫ Soaring high above Gary Neville to win the ball comprehensively in this heading duel as Wales pour forward in wave after glorious wave of attacks on the England goal . . .

In my dreams! In the real world we hardly ever made it into their half, let alone laid siege to their goal. It's true to say, though, that there were no holds barred when Nev and I ran up against each other. We both went in hard for every challenge, but England were so dominant that for most of the time it was me marking him rather than the other way round.

>> I've known some gloomy moments with Wales, but this time the doleful expression is misleading. I was lining up at White Hart Lane in September 2006 for a friendly against Brazil, thus fulfilling my lifetime ambition of taking to the field with the fabulous South Americans. I had been due to face them once before at the Millennium, in the stadium's first game under a closed roof, but I was injured in training and had to pull out at the last minute. The atmosphere that night was sensational and I was gutted to be confined to the stands. This made up for it, though. We lost 2–0 but we played really well, and actually might have won.

⌄ Absorbing instructions from Wales boss John Toshack on the day I knew my international days were drawing to a close. We were in the process of losing a European Championship qualifier to the Republic of Ireland at Croke Park, Dublin, and I felt we were going nowhere. Worse still from a personal point of view, I believed I could give nothing more to the cause. That day I was rubbish, the team were rubbish and we went down to an Irish side we really should have beaten.

As for Tosh, there were initial reservations about his appointment within the squad because previously he had given us all a bit of stick during his commentary on certain games, but I ended up getting on well with him. His methods were different to Sparky's. He was much more old-school, but he always championed good, constructive football and I liked some of the things he brought to the team.

⌄ To look at the endless rows of empty seats at the Millennium you might think this was a training session, but actually I'm taking a corner during a European Championship qualifier against San Marino in March 2007. When the players walk out to be greeted by wide open spaces instead of a roaring crowd it's an eerie experience which does have a dampening effect on the spirits. I suppose the desolate scene offered proof positive that the team was not doing well. If we'd been flying we'd have been pulling in gates of more than 50,000, even for the likes of San Marino. Over the course of two or three years of Sparky's reign, we had the highest attendances in Europe, thanks to the Millennium's capacity. There is a miserable flip side to having such a vast stadium, though, as these deserted stands illustrate all too vividly.

« I knew it was going to be my last appearance for Wales and I wanted to enjoy it. Most of all, I was desperate to go out on a winning note, but in the end had to settle for a goalless draw in our European Championship qualifier against the Czech Republic at the Millennium Stadium in June 2007.

I think I played pretty well, we all did, but I should have scored and it rankled that I missed the chance. Still, it was an emotional occasion in front of more than 30,000 fans, a lot of whom appeared to have turned up especially to see me play my final game for my country. Did the encouraging team performance give me pause for thought about retiring? No, because I had made up my mind that if I wanted to prolong my United career – and I never had the slightest doubt that I did – then the international commitment was just too much for a player in his mid-thirties. I knew there were plenty of promising youngsters coming through, and so it was time to leave.

⌄ Although over the years the media had criticised me for missing friendlies, generally the Welsh public had supported me loyally from the moment I got into the team, and that continued to the end – demonstrated by these placards. And, no, that's not my mum and the rest of the family waving them in the air. At least, I don't think so . . .

CHAPTER FIFTEEN

Top priority

>> My grandmother – always Nannie to me –
has been one of my most loyal and enthusiastic
supporters ever since I started kicking a ball.
Here she's congratulating me with a hug after
I had captained England to victory over Wales
in a schoolboy international at the Vetch Field,
Swansea. The players' entrance is just out of
shot on the right, and I found it remarkable
that there were houses so close to the ground.
Nannie was always a keen fan of football in
general and Manchester United in particular
– she loved watching Sir Matt Busby's great
teams and players, especially George Best.

>> I have always been family-based and that will never change. Snapped
with me here on my twenty-first birthday are, left to right, Aunty Tracy, my
mum Lynne, my grandad, Nannie and Aunty Hayley. Mum has been a
rock for me throughout my life, offering me total encouragement every
step of the way, coming to pretty well every game I ever played, home and

away, right back to my under-ten days. She was always there for me, and I couldn't have asked for more. Grandad still comes to nearly every United home game, travelling by coach from Cardiff and often not getting home until three or four in the morning. Since retiring as a policeman, he has looked after my fan mail, too. Probably he didn't reckon on that particular job lasting so long!

⌃ My dad, Danny Wilson, in action as a stand-off for Cardiff Rugby Club in the mid-1970s. He was my hero as I was growing up and I learned so much from him about what it takes to be a professional sportsman, the playing, the training, the whole bit. He was a star where we lived, both in Cardiff and later in Swinton, for whom he played Rugby League. I was proud to be his son because he was such a fabulous performer, even if perhaps he never quite realised his full potential. People still come up to me in the street to ask me if I realise how exceptional he was, so quick and perfectly balanced. My answer is always the same: I watched him for ten years and, yes, I know he was something special.

≫ It might not sound especially romantic, but Stacey and I got married after training on a Friday morning in September 2007. It was the weekend of an international break, a few months after my last game for Wales, and everything worked out perfectly.

Stacey wanted a quiet wedding, which was fine by me, so we decided to tie the knot in front of only a dozen people, just family and close friends. When I'd finished at Carrington I linked up with my best man – Stuart Grimshaw, a lad I met when playing boys football for Deans all those years ago – and we headed for the ceremony at the Lowry Hotel in Manchester, which is managed by another good mate of mine, Jason Harding.

He took care of everything, amazingly keeping it so quiet that I didn't get a call from the press office until afterwards. It helped that Stacey's aunt was a registrar, and we were able to enjoy a blissfully private day before setting off for Marbella. Of course, we weren't away for long, because there were some big games coming up . . .

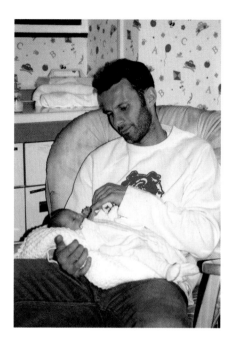

« Cradling my first-born, Libby, in the special care unit at Hope Hospital in Salford. She arrived prematurely by eight weeks and weighed only four pounds at birth, so we couldn't take her home as soon as we would have liked. Of course, it was worrying, but the staff and facilities at the hospital were fantastic, so our minds were quickly eased. Libby made her entrance midweek during April 2003, a few days before United won 6–2 at Newcastle, with me contributing one of the goals. It wasn't a bad week, really!

⋙ On holiday with Libby in Portugal in 2007. Obviously, I'd been talking to her . . .

« My daughter Libby's got a chocolate medal round her neck and I've got a real one as we head for our lap of honour at Old Trafford after the presentation of the Premiership trophy following the West Ham game in May 2007. This family stroll has become a club tradition at the end of the season, whether we're the champions or not, and I approve of it. The kids watch you play all year and it's great for them to go on to the pitch where all the action happens. Libby, who was four at the time of this picture, has never been overawed by the atmosphere and it looks as if baby Zach is of the same mind. Our wives don't join us on the grass and that definitely suits Stacey. She's much happier to be on the sidelines taking the pictures.

⟱ Zach was asked to say 'cheese' before this snap at a skating show at the Manchester Evening News Arena. He complied with enthusiasm.

CHAPTER SIXTEEN

1991–2010

Colours of
my life

⌐ Wearing the Manchester United shirt during my twenty years at the club has been like running around with a rainbow on my back. Far from being limited to the traditional plain red, there has been an amazing variety of colours and designs. Some of them I love, others I'm not so fond of, but without doubt my favourite is the red top with the laced collar which we wore when we lifted the first Premier League title in 1992/93. Of course, that carried the extra significance of ending United's twenty-six years in the championship wilderness, so everything about that season is unforgettable. We kept it for the following campaign, too, when we achieved our first league and FA Cup double, so I guess my affection for it is hardly surprising.

I wasn't quite so keen on the green-and-gold third kit of that era, although it was really different, almost eccentric for the time, and it had an historical association with our predecessor club, Newton Heath. Of course come 2010 those colours had a rather more controversial connotation. Round about 1993, too, we debuted our first all-black kit, which I thought was very classy. Another popular one with me was the 1999 Champions League shirt. Perhaps I imagined it, but there always seemed to be an extra depth to the red, which appeared almost to shine, maybe because it was usually under the lights when we wore it.

Often I like a shirt because of the fit and the feel. For example, the much-derided blue-and-white 'J-cloth' from the 1992 League Cup final was fine by me because it felt good and was a fairly narrow fit. I wasn't so happy with most of the baggy styles; then there were a few which I just didn't like the look of – for example, the infamous grey effort from 1996/97, the broad blue-and-white stripes from the previous campaign and, much later, the horizontal blue pinstripe.

At first I wasn't a great fan of the new design for 2009/10, with the deep 'V' to echo a United kit of the 1920s, but I must admit it has grown on me. Of course, winning a trophy always helps, and although the Premiership slipped away on the final day of the season, our League Cup triumph ensured that we didn't end up empty-handed.

As for the debate about whether the constant changing of shirts is fair to our fans, it should be pointed out that people do enjoy them enormously. Many supporters wear their football shirts to school, to play in, even for best gear, so they do get their money's worth over the year or two that the shirt is current. If people wore any other garment of a similar price as often, there wouldn't be any complaints. Also, the replica can save a lot of agonising over Christmas or birthday presents. After all, you can hardly go wrong with a United shirt for a United supporter! I don't think there's any doubt that the replica shirt is here to stay. It's replaced the traditional scarf as a way of showing your club's colours and proclaiming your loyalty. These days it is worn by people of all ages and walks of life.

In the end, I'm proud to wear the shirt whatever its shade or design. There's only one thing about it that truly matters to me – that it bears the badge of Manchester United, the only club I have ever wanted to play for.

Acknowledgements

My family, for their unwavering support
Sir Alex Ferguson, for his generous (and occasionally imaginative!) foreword
Harry Swales, for everything
Also, for finding such nice things to say about me and not taking the mick too much: Bryan Robson, Paul Ince, Gary Pallister, Lee Sharpe, Steve Bruce, Paul Scholes, Gary Neville, Phil Neville, David Beckham, Ole Gunnar Solskjaer, John O'Shea, Wayne Rooney, Sir Bobby Charlton, Brian Kidd, Ian Rush.

Ryan's collaborator, Ivan Ponting, would like to thank:
Pat, Rosie and Joe Ponting, always there, always positive
Rhea Halford of Headline, for her expert and enlightened editing
Jo Whitford, also of Headline
Jacqui Caulton for her designs
Cliff Butler, the fount of all Old Trafford wisdom
Andy Cowie of Colorsport, John Peters of Manchester United and Getty Images, Hayley Newman at Getty Images, Lucie Gregory at the Press Association, David Scripps at Mirrorpix, Billy Robertson at Action Images, Mark Leech at Offside.
Marcella Keane
Mark Wylie and Nicola Struthers at the Manchester United Museum
Karen Shotbolt of Manchester United
Les Gold
David Welch

To order a copy of *Memories Never Die* by Del Deanus, please send a cheque made payable to Emma Luscombe for £12.99 (price includes postage and packaging) to 22 Lockleys Drive, Welwyn, Hertfordshire, AL6 9LU. All profits will go to the Motor Neurone Disease Association.

Picture credits

Action Images

9, 11 (below), 17, 20 (above), 22 (below), 28, 29, 32, 33, 34, 44, 48, 65, 88, 92, 107 (above left), 107 (middle), 114, 115, 116, 119, 132, 145, 147, 150, 152, 153, 170, 176, 178, 179, 185, 187 (above), 188, 190, 191, 193, 197, 198, 201 (below), 209 (above), 218, 225, 239, 241, 246, 277, 278 (above), 279, 281

Charles Green Portraits

207

Cliff Butler, Manchester United

14, 15, 18–19,

Colorsport

16, 25, 26, 46, 49, 50, 54 (above), 61, 63, 76 (above left), 87, 89, 94, 103, 105, 117, 118, 128, 133, 144, 148 (left), 148 (right), 155, 156, 157, 166, 167, 219, 221, 224, 234, 250, 271 (above), 275, 278 (below)

Getty Images

4, 8, 35, 37, 42, 43, 45, 47, 52, 54 (below), 64, 67, 70, 74, 77 (above), 77 (below), 81, 90, 101, 107 (below), 111, 112, 122, 125, 126, 127, 129, 131, 135, 136, 146, 149, 151, 154, 160, 161, 163, 165, 168, 169, 171, 174–75, 180, 181, 184, 187 (below), 189, 192, 195, 196, 201 (above), 204, 205, 206, 208, 209 (below), 212, 213, 214, 215, 217, 220 (left), 220 (right), 222–23, 226, 227, 228, 235, 236, 237, 240, 242, 243, 245, 247, 249, 253, 256, 260, 266, 270, 272, 276, 280, 293, 296

Courtesy of Les Gold

261

Marcella Keane

265

Mirrorpix

271 (below)

Offside

11 (above), 20 (below), 22 (above), 24, 27, 60, 62, 69, 78, 79, 91, 107 (above right), 108, 162, 177, 200, 251, 258, 259, 267

Press Association Images

1, 10, 21, 23, 36, 38, 40, 41, 56, 57, 66, 68, 72–73, 76 (above right), 76 (below), 84, 85, 86, 93, 95, 96, 97, 100, 104, 106, 113, 124, 130, 134, 137, 138, 139, 140, 141, 164, 172–73, 185, 194, 199, 211, 216, 229, 233, 238, 252, 257, 262, 263, 273, 274, 285, 289 (above)

Reebok International Limited

75

Courtesy of Ryan Giggs

232, 284 (above), 284 (below), 286, 287, 288 (above), 288 (below), 289 (below)

Pages 294–295 (Left to right, top to bottom)

Top: Colorsport, PA, PA, PA, Getty Images, PA, Getty Images, Getty Images.
Middle: Getty Images, Getty Images, Action Images, Getty Images, Colorsport, PA, Action Images, Getty Images, PA, Action Images, Getty Images, Action Images, Action Images, Action Images, Action Images, PA.
Bottom: Getty Images, PA, Colorsport, PA, PA, PA, Offside, Getty Images.